WOMAN SPIRIT
AWAKENING IN NATURE

GROWING INTO THE FULLNESS
OF WHO YOU ARE

NANCY BARRETT CHICKERNEO, PhD

FOREWORD BY EILEEN FISHER

Walking Together, Finding the Way ®
SKYLIGHT PATHS ®
PUBLISHING
Woodstock, Vermont

Woman Spirit Awakening in Nature:
Growing Into the Fullness of Who You Are

2008 Quality Paperback Edition, First Printing
© 2008 by Nancy Barrett Chickerneo

For information regarding permission to reprint material from this book, please mail or fax your request in writing to SkyLight Paths Publishing, Permissions Department, at the address / fax number listed below or e-mail your request to permissions@skylightpaths.com.

Page 182 constitutes a continuation of this copyright page.

Library of Congress Cataloging-in-Publication Data
Chickerneo, Nancy Barrett.
Woman spirit awakening in nature : growing into the fullness of who you are / by Nancy Barrett Chickerneo ; foreword by Eileen Fisher.
p. cm.
Includes bibliographical references.
ISBN-13: 978-1-59473-250-8 (quality pbk.)
ISBN-10: 1-59473-250-7 (quality pbk.)
1. Women—Religious life. 2. Nature—Religious aspects. I. Title.
BL625.7.C455 2008
204'.4082—dc22

2008025799

10   9   8   7   6   5   4   3   2   1
Manufactured in Canada
Cover design: Shanti Durkee
Cover art and interior illustrations: Nancy Barrett Chickerneo

SkyLight Paths Publishing is creating a place where people of different spiritual traditions come together for challenge and inspiration, a place where we can help each other understand the mystery that lies at the heart of our existence.

SkyLight Paths sees both believers and seekers as a community that increasingly transcends traditional boundaries of religion and denomination—people wanting to learn from each other, *walking together, finding the way.*

SkyLight Paths, "Walking Together, Finding the Way," and colophon are trademarks of LongHill Partners, Inc., registered in the U.S. Patent and Trademark Office.

Walking Together, Finding the Way®
Published by SkyLight Paths Publishing
A Division of Longhill Partners, Inc.
Sunset Farm Offices, Route 4, P.O. Box 237
Woodstock, VT 05091
Tel: (802) 457-4000 Fax: (802) 457-4004
www.skylightpaths.com

I dedicate this book to

The Artist in whom

I experience abundant life.

There is no creation that does not have radiance.

Be it greenness or seed, blossom or beauty, it could not be creation without it.

—HILDEGARD OF BINGEN, 12TH CENTURY

Contents

CONTENTS

Foreword

When my friend Nancy first asked me to write a foreword for her book, I felt a bit anxious. I don't write. I design clothes! In that particular moment, I was feeling a little sad and a bit stuck. It had been a long winter. As I began to read her book, I was pulled into it and reminded of the fun we've had as SPA Sisters, the brilliant work she does, and how deeply I have been touched by it. Nancy has created a profoundly easy pathway to knowing your true self through applying simple methods and the amazing healing quality of nature.

As I continued to read *Woman Spirit Awakening in Nature* and deal with my winter struggles, I asked myself, "Why don't I do what Nancy suggests?" I grabbed my blanket, opened the door, and went out on my front porch. As I sat there, I was struck (literally) by the blustery, gusty winds of the day and had to ask, "What is nature saying to me?" Even in my stuck state, the wind had its effect: It held the promise that spring was coming. Out of my contracted winter state of mind, I was reminded that I have a wilder, more playful side that, like spring, is waiting to emerge. I remembered that these phases of dormancy are important. For me, they can be times to step back and regroup, to create a space so that the tender green shoots of spring can appear. And I realized I felt somehow comforted, hopeful, and freer as I headed back into the house.

I am thankful to live in the joy and lightness of my friend Nancy. We have very different spiritual perspectives, and yet through nature we are each able to continuously rediscover ourselves and to connect to that deeper knowing. Nature provides a mirror for each of us to see who we are and models the confidence to believe in what we see.

Read this wonderful book, open the door, go outside....

EILEEN FISHER

Beginning

We were a group of busy women, managing work and life, who decided nevertheless to make time to meet in a restful place where we could explore and share our lives with one another. With nature as our setting, we would gather periodically for several days in various places around the country, behaving as though we had all the time in the world. Our time together was like a spa for the mind and the spirit. We laughed, we talked, we danced, we played, we walked on the beach, we journaled, we drew pictures, we tried on clothes. It was great fun. Best of all, we each came to see ourselves more clearly and to connect with each other more deeply.

Each time we got together, we went outdoors. And each time, we discovered that nature offered an amazing variety of metaphors that symbolized our hopes and longings, our problems and solutions, our wisdom and spirit. As we shared the nature metaphors we found, we began to share our deeper, spiritual selves, and we grew into a fuller sense of ourselves.

We knew we were on to something.

We decided to call ourselves the SPA Sisters—for Spirit, Place, and Authentic Self. (At first, we thought about calling ourselves the SPAS, but thankfully someone came up with adding the "isters" part!) Eventually we began dreaming of creating a space where other women could experience the joy and awareness that we were finding in nature and in each other.

Out of these simple beginnings, the SPA Sisters Program emerged, with one primary goal: to give women a space to be in nature, using creative tools for reflection. The basic structure of the program includes a one-day Awakening Retreat and a six-part Wellspring Group. The process is, literally, down to earth: we use nature as our place and we choose metaphors from nature that resonate with us to see ourselves more clearly. There are only three basic requirements of participants: quiet down in nature; be aware of your senses and what you are attracted to; stay present to this until you understand what meaning it has for your life. We also encourage the use of journaling and creative tools for expression, and sharing with others who are on a similar journey. But the bottom line is this: No experience necessary. All are welcome. You can be a SPA Sister wherever you find nature. You can undertake the experience on your own or with a friend or a group.

When fueled by beauty and sensuality, our relationship with the visible world may move our hearts.

—LAURA SEWALL,
ECOPSYCHOLOGY

2

The book you are holding in your hand, *Woman Spirit Awakening in Nature,* is your invitation to experience this life-energizing process for yourself. Each chapter is based on one aspect of the SPA Sisters Awakening Retreat or Wellspring Group. At the conclusion of each chapter you will find an exercise designed to deepen your experience in nature and your learning about yourself. You may want to journey through these chapters by yourself at your own pace, or with a dear friend or sister, or with a group of women you gather together. (You may also want to come to a SPA Sisters event—you'll always be welcome! For more information, see the Welcoming section at the back of the book.)

One of the ways to enliven any SPA Sisters event is to let women share their stories. In keeping with that tradition, other women and I will share our experiences with you in this book, to keep you company and provide you with community. I'll start by telling you a bit of my story. I am a psychotherapist and have worked in the mental health field for over twenty years. Even in my earlier years of doing pastoral counseling, I often designed and facilitated retreats and workshops outdoors, in nature. Gradually, I began noticing how much this magnificent landscape around us mirrors who we are as part of creation and I wondered why nature was so under-utilized in our traditional healing process. I was seeing women grow and learn on one-day retreats as much as they might in months of therapy. I became convinced that our emotional and spiritual health is related to our relationship with the rest of nature.

Lest you think that I grew up as "nature woman," let me be quick to say that wasn't the case. I had a difficult childhood. Instead of enjoying a childlike relationship with nature, I focused on the serious matters of life. I decided I was an atheist, and it wasn't until age thirty that I came to believe in God. As I opened to my spiritual self, nature became a rich source of spiritual nurture. In the time since, I have learned and grown and known peace and grace at my core. My work now focuses on ways to help women grow into their fullness through nature, to re-access the wonder of who they are, and to find their own path of spiritual growth.

All that said, in spite of my professional credentials as a counselor and psychotherapist, I am primarily Nancy, enjoying my life and engaging in my relationships as a wife, mother, grandmother, and friend. And I am deeply pleased to invite you into this new beginning for yourself. The purpose of this book is to help you grow into the fullness of who you are through nature and the nurture of Spirit. Though I draw primarily from a Christian perspective because that is my faith tradition, this book is for women of all faiths and backgrounds. Nature is available for each of us, and I believe that when we allow ourselves to be fully present in it, nature will show us much about our authentic selves and our Creator.

I like to think of it this way: Whenever I paint, in some way I am creating a self-portrait. My work is from me and is therefore an expression of who I am. My exuberant watercolors reveal something of my colorful, clear, free self; my creation mirrors me. The same could be said about nature: All creation reveals The Creator. When you step into nature's realm, you are stepping into a place of awakening, a place where your deepest self can be revealed, including your spiritual core.

As you take this journey inward, I encourage you to use creative tools such as drawing, journaling, or poetry to express yourself. You can use the Journaling section at the back of this

Through nature, the species is introduced to transcendence, in the sense that there is something more going on than the individual. Most people are either awakened to or are strengthened in their spiritual journey by experiences in the natural world.

—RICHARD LOUV,
LAST CHILD IN THE WOODS

book, or a special journal you select, or a simple notebook. The important thing is to have an identified place that is exclusively yours, a place where you can express yourself freely. From the context of my training and experience—my masters in religious studies, with an emphasis on creativity and spirituality; my profession as a watercolor painter; my doctorate in art therapy—I wholeheartedly believe that creative expression, especially in natural settings, can help us live fuller lives. When we reconnect with our senses—with what we see, hear, touch, smell, and taste—that expression comes naturally. No training necessary.

Whether you embark on this exploration on your own or with other women, it is important to create a safe space with no judgment, a space in which all expression and ideas are welcome. If you are undertaking this exploration on your own, you may need to tell your inner critic to "take a hike" so you can be open and fully present to yourself, without criticism. If you're with a group, make it a safe place where each woman can dare to express who she truly is. Be fully present so you can listen to each woman tell her story; leave any advice-giving or fixing urges at the door.

As you read the book and enjoy the experiential suggestions at the end of each chapter, give yourself enough time so you won't feel rushed. Perhaps you could set apart an evening, a Sunday afternoon, or even a whole day for yourself to spend with a chapter. (A typical Awakening Retreat is about six hours, but I've broken that into two chapters in this book to make it more

There is no way in which to understand the world without first detecting it through the radar-net of our senses.

—DIANE ACKERMAN,
A NATURAL HISTORY OF THE SENSES

As you sit on the hill-side, or lie prone under the trees of the forest, or sprawl wet-legged by a mountain stream, the great door, that does not look like a door, opens.

—STEPHEN GRAHAM,
THE GENTLE ART
OF TRAMPING

schedule friendly for everyday life.) Whatever time you set apart for your spirit time, make sure that it is truly *your* time—a time when you can be separate from the demands of daily life and attentive to your needs and personal discovery.

I want to leave one more thought with you before you begin. Perhaps you've had the privilege of reading some of May Sarton's books that reflect her love of nature. She often wrote about her garden, her daily life in New Hampshire, and the seasons. As a keen observer of both her inner and outer world, she was a strong voice for living life to the fullest. In *Journal of a Solitude,* Sarton wrote about being impatient with household tasks, with "things," and in one particular entry, bemoaned the current task facing her—to repaint an old floor:

> Yesterday I tried to get paint, but it will have to be mixed, and it all takes time, "errand time."
> Gardening is altogether different. There the door is always open into the "holy"—growth, birth, death.

That one little line captures the essential gift of nature: the door is always open into the holy. Nature is there for you, waiting to reflect your deepest self back to you and to teach you The Creator's wisdom. A step into nature's embrace is always a step into a richer, fuller life. The door is wide open; come on out!

ONE
Awakening
COMING TO YOUR SENSES

Come Home to the Garden

This is a book about daring ... daring to come back to your roots.

In the midwestern prairie where I lived for nine years, root systems of certain plants go as deep as fifteen feet into the earth. When the season is dry, the plant remains mysteriously green—even under the scorching August sun. This tough ecosystem has been in place for thousands of years, and it took the invention of the steel plow to finally cut through its roots and tame it into farmland. Plants with lesser root systems have long since blown away, looking for open, easy, interrupted dirt to seed in. Yet some of the prairie remains, and many people in the Midwest are actively looking for ways to reclaim and restore it. Women face a similar challenge: we can give way to the plow of technology that tries to tame us; we can dry up and blow away, looking for

The Plains are not forgiving. Anything that is shallow—the easy optimism of a homesteader; the false hope that denies geography, climate, history; the tree whose roots don't reach ground water—will dry up and blow away.

—KATHLEEN NORRIS

open, easy dirt to seed in; or we can root deeply and thrive. It's time for our own reclamation and restoration.

The fact is, we are not just "in nature," we *are* nature! According to Jewish and Christian spiritual tradition, we started out as part of the Garden of Eden. The garden seemed like a good fit for humans, but we wanted more. We wanted to do our own thing. Now we have a whole lot more, but we are no longer sure if we are part of creation or just the creators of the "more." Because we have so much, many of us have forgotten our roots, and this is having a disastrous effect on us and our planet.

As if the Industrial Revolution were not enough to overwhelm us, we are now being buried by the Information Age. As more and more ways to communicate and gather information spin toward us, we are flooded with more expectations than we can handle, more stress than we can live with. But we can't completely check out of this lifestyle; we need a connection with the larger world. My husband, for one, felt e-mails were such a burden that he quit checking them some time ago, but I have noticed that he sheepishly asks me when he needs something from his e-mail account. Imagine: We were created for a garden and we ended up here!

In short, what we have created threatens to engulf us, like an invasive species that was first planted under someone's good intentions but rapidly took over, to the point where it became destructive. The infamous kudzu plant, for example, was introduced at the Philadelphia Exposition in 1876 for livestock forage and as an ornamental plant. Now it blankets everything in its path, growing up to a foot per day, covering and destroying low vegetation, and reaching almost one hundred feet as it grows ferociously up and over trees.

Good intentions turn into stress, and stress into anxieties, depression, and addictions—as my booming work as a therapist attests. Even therapists are stressed out. We not only share the burden of others, but we also have to go to battle with the insurance companies over payment. Our modern culture has created quite a mess, and it is time to come home to the garden.

Whether your tradition tells of the Garden of Eden or a different creation story, our common origin is that we started out as part of nature, walking the ground and knowing the land. We learned about other creatures and plants and we knew who liked to eat whom. We were, literally, grounded.

Gradually, we began to "improve" our lot, and now many in the United States own several televisions, three-car garages for at least two cars, even second homes. And, of course, we are working longer hours to pay for all of this. Have you noticed that once you accumulate something, it gradually begins to seem necessary? As we become more and more tired, sometimes too exhausted to do anything other than watch television, we get caught in the cycle of the media telling us what else we need to own, which only increases our need to work more to pay for it. Think about this: Reality shows about survival try to show us how hard it is to live in primitive circumstances. In truth, I think

I go to nature to be soothed and healed, and to have my senses put in order.

—JOHN BURROUGHS,
THE GOSPEL OF NATURE

it is more difficult to survive in our fast-moving, high-frequency culture.

This is one of the reasons the growing field of ecopsychology has caught my attention. The basic ideas of ecopsychology are that we, as organic beings, are part of a wider natural world that affects our health, emotions, and relationships, and that nature can teach us much about harmony, balance, timelessness, and stability.

The Wilds of Yourself

The term *ecopsychology* originated with the book *The Voice of the Earth,* where editor Theodore Roszak makes the profound statement, "The Earth's cry for rescue ... is our own cry for a scale and quality of life that will free each of us to become the complete person we were born to be." Ecopsychology is based on the concept that, at the deepest level, we are bonded to the earth "that mothered us into existence," and that we can awaken our inherent reciprocity with nature.

This idea of unity with the earth is not new, of course. A wide variety of ancient and modern cultures have histories of embracing nature. Nature-based cultures are particularly interesting to me because they live with a conscious respect for and interdependence with the earth that many of us in modern cultures have lost. The Okanagan people, for example, are a Native American tribe spanning the Pacific Northwest from

Feminist ecopsychology understands that in bonding with the natural world, ecstatic states of celebration and interconnection are unleashed— experiences that, in modern society, are repressed in ourselves and oppressed in others.

—MARY GOMES,
ECOCPSYCHOLOGY

Washington up into Canada. Jeanette Armstrong, an Okanagan Canadian author, speaks of her people's reverent connection with the earth:

> The way we act in our human capacity has significant effects on the Earth because it is said that we are the hands of the spirit, in that we can fashion Earth pieces with that knowledge and therefore transform the Earth. It is our most powerful potential, and so we are told that we are responsible for the Earth.

If we traverse the centuries, we find many spiritual forerunners who believed that Spirit is revealed through nature. David, the shepherd boy who slew the giant Goliath and went on to be Israel's king, wrote these words:

> *The heavens declare the glory of God;*
> *the skies proclaim the work of his hands.*
> *Day after day they pour forth speech;*
> *night after night they display knowledge.*
> *There is no speech or language*
> *where their voice is not heard.*
> *Their voice goes out into all the earth,*
> *their words to the ends of the world.*
> *   (Psalm 19:1–4 NIV)*

My book, O Philosopher, is the nature of created things, and any time I wish to read the words of God, the book is before me.

—SAINT ANTHONY

11

Paul the apostle, writing from the first century, also saw nature as revealing of God: "From the time the world was created, people have seen the earth and sky and all that God made. They can clearly see [God's] invisible qualities—[God's] eternal power and divine nature" (Romans 1:20, NLT).

Saint Francis, born in the twelfth century, saw God in nature, especially in birds and animals. Today he is considered the saint for all creatures and the environment. In *The Lessons of St. Francis,* John Michael Talbot writes, "The key to understanding this unusual saint's unique approach to the cosmos is this: If God made it, Francis adored it. All created things were part of God's big family, and through the adoration of the things God had made, Francis felt an exhilaration that was both rooted and soaring, both worldly and spiritual."

Julian of Norwich, a fourteenth-century mystic and the first woman writing in English of whom we have a record, speaks across the centuries of her reverence for creation: "Our Lord desires that our spirit be truly turned to gaze upon him and upon all his glorious creation, for it is exceedingly good."

The lively philosopher, biologist, and Jesuit priest Teilhard de Chardin shared his creation-centered spirituality in the twentieth century. His words seem an appropriate message for our time: "Our own age seems primarily to need a rejuvenation of supernatural forces to be effected by driving roots deeply into the nutritious energies of the earth."

To one who has been
long in city pent,
'Tis very sweet to look
into the fair
And open face of
heaven,—to breathe
a prayer
Full in the smile of the
blue firmament.

—JOHN KEATS

These days it's politically correct to be respectful of the earth, to be ecological, to participate in ways to save our planet. Here in the Midwest, prairie restoration projects are all the rage—and delightfully so. While some still believe soybeans and corn are native to this huge landscape, others who know that these plants are actually newcomers to the land are gradually recognizing the importance of restoring the prairie. Bit by bit, it is coming back. Not only does this restoration respect what has existed in this ecosystem for many millennia, it also is key to bringing back the beautiful black soil of the heartland.

It is amazing to think that the prairie ecosystem was so devalued by the first settlers that their main effort was to create a way to destroy it, which the steel plow finally accomplished. Now, the strength and vulnerability of waves of tall grass prairie are finally being understood for their true beauty and resilience. The gradual renewal of the prairie ecosystem has much to teach us about restoring our own inherent beauty and reclaiming our truest selves.

If you are ready to come into a deeper understanding and ownership of the wildness and wonder of your truest self, nature can lead you there. Are you ready to reclaim the prairie of your soul—all of you, including the parts you are ashamed of, dislike, or maybe aren't even aware of at this point, the parts you thought were extinct? Are you ready to bring back the vanishing prairie grasses and wildflowers, the natural treasures that I like to call "the wilds of yourself"?

Well-behaved women seldom make history.

—LAUREL THATCHER ULRICH

What would the world
be, once bereft
Of wet and wildness?
Let them be left,
O let them be left,
wildness and wet,
Long live the weeds and
the wildness yet.

—GERARD MANLEY
HOPKINS

As women, many of us have worked for years to appear "tame," with our decorated homes and well-coifed hair, but at our core there is a wildness, a vitality, an aliveness waiting to emerge. Clarissa Pinkola Estes's book *Women Who Run with the Wolves* hit a nerve for women in the nineties who wanted to get back to their wild core. She wrote:

> Healthy wolves and healthy women share certain psychic characteristics: keen sensing, playful spirit, and a heightened capacity for devotion. Wolves and women are relational by nature, inquiring, possessed of great endurance and strength. They are deeply intuitive, intensely concerned with their young, their mate, and their pack. They are experienced in adapting to constantly changing circumstances; they are fiercely stalwart and very brave.... A woman's issues of soul cannot be treated by carving her into a more acceptable form as defined by an unconscious culture.

Where does your wildness surface? Perhaps it is a gnawing feeling that something is missing. Or maybe it bubbles up as an urge to do *something* to get out of the rut you're in. Or maybe you are experiencing an emerging passion, a sprout of creativity that is ready to grow into something more.

What would happen if you decided to seriously consider how a closer relationship with the earth could restore your spiritual and emotional life to health? What could you discover about your natural wild core? What remnants would you find to work with? If you are passionate about the retrieval of your true self, it's time to get out there, to get out into nature to rediscover and reclaim the person you were created to be.

"Get Out There!"

During the years I worked as an art therapist in a drug rehabilitation center, I struggled to find a way to help people access that deeper, wilder part of themselves, to regain a sense of their own spirituality. The clients were all required to be part of a 12-step group while in treatment, which brought them face-to-face with step 2: "Came to believe a power greater than myself could restore me to sanity." Client after client would tell me of their hopelessness about finding a higher power after difficult experiences with organized religion. I would often ask them to put aside the big-*G* thoughts for a moment and remember a time in their lives when they felt peaceful. I was astonished that almost 100 percent of them reported that their experiences of peace were in nature: "In the wilderness of Wyoming" or "On a mountain in Colorado." I began to wonder why we were meeting in the concrete-block basement of an old schoolhouse.

We started to go outside. It's where awakening to our wild self, our full nature, can truly begin.

The more I worked with addiction clients, and the more we went outdoors, the more a dream grew to further this work on the land rather than in a building. My husband, Leon, and I were able to purchase twenty-one acres of land we named Prairie Lake so I could continue the work with more women. During the transition,

Many forms of pleasure that have been numbed by urban living, from bodily to perceptual to aesthetic to spiritual, come back to life in natural settings.

—MARY GOMES,
ECOPSYCHOLOGY

doors opened for us, making it possible to find the property, sell our house, and build the Prairie Lake house. What I had not counted on was the immense shift within myself after moving to the country. I am an extrovert, and that's a hard way to be on twenty-one acres. I was stuck. My husband and I were both exhausted after building the house and moving, and I felt alone. During the first month of our country life, I acted as if I were still living in the suburbs, and my telephone bill was embarrassingly high. (This was long before "anywhere, anytime" unlimited minutes!)

This was the beginning of a different kind of life for me. Eventually, I grew tired of moping around and began to go outside and walk the property. Back in my suburban home, my route had usually been from house to garage to wherever and back again, with very little contact with nature. Spending intentional time outside was like breaking through to another dimension. I felt as if I were waking up.

I started to dig in the dirt, and I created a perennial garden. Much to my surprise, this brought a huge sense of satisfaction. I can still feel the warming in my chest ... sort of a puffed-up contentment. I started out wearing garden gloves, but they flew off my hands in minutes. I longed for direct contact with the dirt. I loved the carefree sensation of digging, smoothing, piling the soil. My hands got scraped and scratched, and I could barely get the dirt out from under my fingernails. But it didn't matter. I felt as if I were a child making mud pies. I felt free!

When we first moved to the country, I had assumed I would be most interested in the lake, but I found myself being drawn more and more to the prairie. It was planted with soybeans when we arrived, but as my husband and I brainstormed possibilities, we decided to start a prairie restoration project with native Illinois seeds gathered from remnants. I thought it sounded fun—even noble—but I didn't know I was going to fall in love.

I began waking up, for the first time since childhood, to the fact that nature could keep me company, and that very often it was company enough. It allowed me to finally, blessedly, come home to my "natural" self.

That first year, the prairie was short, with black-eyed Susans dominating. By the third year, the prairie was a thick jungle, as tall as I was and difficult to walk through. I dragged my paints, paper, and a beach chair out to the land, to be engulfed in the prairie, and I felt at home. I spent untold hours wandering and painting what I saw, and I started to identify with many parts of the natural world I roamed in. As I studied the ancient compass plants, growing ten to twelve feet tall, I began to feel sturdier, stronger, and in some way, more solid. As I contemplated their root systems—fifteen-foot roots that allowed them to survive the prairie burns and come back up with tough new stalks—I thought of my own deep roots in God that allowed me to survive the "burns" of my childhood wounds.

I loved the giant leathery leaves of the prairie dock plant, and I felt gratitude for the tenacity I had gained from both the suffering

There is something infinitely healing in the repeated refrains of nature—the assurance that dawn comes after night, and spring after the winter.

—RACHEL CARSON

17

and the joy of my life. I could identify with the unselfconsciousness of the purple coneflower, raised up for all to see. The gentle movement of the prairie grasses waving in the wind called to me, inviting a softer edge to my personality. The big sky, black as pitch at night, with occasional crashing thunderstorms and brilliant lightning bolts illuminating it, helped me recognize my humanness—and my need for God.

As I painted, the sun beat down on my straw hat and my freckles leapt to the surface. Interesting bugs walked over my paper, and I found myself fascinated by their beauty and character. I especially liked the bright green luminescent beetles—and to think that I hated bugs in the house in my suburban life! It was a literal wonder to find myself as a mature adult being reunited with the fullness and creativity of my child self, a part of me I had assumed no longer existed.

The truth is, it's very difficult to see our complete selves clearly, if at all. We get tangled up in our complexities, attitudes, and judgments. We live in our bodies, looking out and seeing other people's faces, but we can't truly see our own. We see ourselves better with the help of a "mirror." The people in our lives mirror us back, reflecting what they see in us, but the picture is not always clear. And if our mirrors are broken, the reflection we receive is distorted. Occasionally, someone in our lives mirrors the truth about who we are, but good mirrors are hard to find.

Nature is one mirror we can always count on; it can reflect back our true selves with clarity and reveal the parts of ourselves

When we identify creatures, objects, or processes in the natural world that resemble us in personality, we are afforded the opportunity to glean who we are in the deepest psychological and spiritual sense … all are like mirrors in which we can see and study ourselves.

—Philip Chard,
The Healing Earth

we have numbed or hidden. When I first moved to the country, I rejoiced in the panoramic views. Very soon, however, the vastness of nature began to feel lonely and overwhelming. It wasn't until much later that I could see how the open space mirrored the unfilled place inside of me that I wasn't yet ready to look at.

When we are ready to look, nature is ready to be our mirror.

Come to Your Senses

When women gather for a SPA Sisters Awakening Retreat, one of the first exercises we ask them to do is go out into nature (whatever the weather!) and look for something that attracts them, something they see as precious or valuable. Mary Fisher later told me that she had been afraid she wouldn't find anything she felt attracted to and admitted she had come up with a back-up plan in case she found nothing. Her experience of returning that day in a blush of excitement over what she found is one I've seen over and over again—and have had myself, many times. It is an experience that is waiting for you.

My colleague Marie Swanson Egeland, who created Intermission Therapies in Geneva, Illinois, and the tour company I Travel, has had to spend most of her life indoors because of severe allergies. On a SPA Sisters Retreat, she took a chance and decided to go outdoors:

Go to the winter woods: Listen there. Look. Watch, and the "dead months" will give you a subtler secret than any you have found in the forest.

—FIONA MACLEOD
(1855–1905)

19

Re-enchantment is the word that captures my rediscovery of nature more than forty years after being "driven indoors." Our group had gathered at dusk on a November evening, meeting indoors before bundling up to trek the short distance to nearby Island Park. It had begun snowing just before we left the building. From indoors, the snow looked like confetti thrown during a parade.

The snow wafted soft, but fast, and quite soon we were all part of the white landscape. We had started out as a color spectrum of coats, but we were now head-to-toe white, as though we had donned liturgical vestments. Our humanity melded with the snowscape, and the resulting autonomy led to a cocoon-like insulation, where I felt safe to release my soul. As the snow continued to fall and was rapidly erasing human footprints, the internal balance of nature was inspiring a spiritual awakening in me.

I thought of the movie about a neurologist's experience with awakening a ward full of people who emerged, albeit for a short period, from chronic comas. In some way, I, too, was coming out of a "coma" in which I had been deprived of the power of nature on a sensory level. My nerve endings still tingle at that miraculous experience.

No matter whether you have picked up this book out of curiosity or longing—or even skepticism—I make the same statement to you that I make to every SPA Sisters retreat participant: when you place yourself in nature's embrace, stay open to the possibility of something new and unexpected.

I have to smile a bit, thinking about what happened when I took my own advice. My friend Eileen Fisher, a great supporter of the SPA Sisters, asked me to facilitate a retreat for her and her five sisters, and I wanted it to be especially wonderful because they were my friends. However, the March weather did not live up to my expectations of a peaceful day in nature. It was cold and damp, with fifty-mile-an-hour winds. I went straight to The Weather Maker with my complaints and then reluctantly bundled up to go outside for my first walk of the retreat, to find what attracted me in nature and what it said about me.

As I walked into Island Park, I was aware of the crashing sound of the river as the waves appeared to be going almost backward. My damp hair kept flying against my cheeks, and I wondered how I could possibly find something precious or valuable in the midst of this maelstrom. I had to start by expressing my annoyance:

> *Noise, river rushing by,*
> *Wind blowing, hair flying,*
> *Dark clouds,*
> *Where are you, God?*

I felt incrementally better after unloading my angst on God, and was able to shake off a little of my misery so I could actually be open to what might be available to me beyond the weather—or maybe within it. Having finished my prayer, I looked up at the whirling clouds and noticed a hawk that appeared white against the dark sky. It was slowly doing figure eights, apparently not disturbed by the weather. I was attracted to—actually, riveted to—the sight. I realized that I was fascinated by the hawk's

Nature—the sublime, the harsh, and the beautiful—offers ... an environment where [we] can easily contemplate infinity and eternity.

—RICHARD LOUV,
LAST CHILD IN THE WOODS

21

steadiness and steadfastness in the midst of rough weather, and was suddenly aware that I had those qualities in me. I felt humbled and grateful, and I finished my morning retreat with a sketch of the soaring hawk in the rough sky—and another poem.

> *River rushing by,*
> *Wind blowing harsh,*
> *Hawk still gliding even on this day.*

Another retreat participant, Deb Marqui, who works as a social worker and now facilitates SPA Sisters retreats and workshops, had a very different experience on her first retreat. For her, the sun shone and the breezes were gentle. As she took in the earthy, fresh smell of the air, a lone duck in the river caught her attention. Tuning into what she felt drawn to, she reflected in her journal:

> *A duck stands on an exposed slippery rock*
> *on one foot and yawns,*
> *completely balanced as the river swirls around the rock.*
> *As my life happens and flows by rapidly, and often "slippery,"*
> *am I as balanced and confident?*
> *I think not.*
> *I am being called to stretch myself.*

One of the principles of SPA Sisters is that what we are attracted to in nature reveals a part of ourselves. For Deb, the duck balanced on the rock mirrored some of her own need for balance. What might nature be waiting to mirror to you about your life, about your qualities, about your needs?

Before you dash out the door to find out, there are two more things we need to talk about. The first is your "be perfect" side. (Yes, I suspect you have one; most of us do.) Here's how I see this: In Genesis, when God created everything and then finally us, God pronounced us "very good." Not excellent. Not perfect. We got only a B+, not an A. For me, that is very good news. The B+ releases us from the demand to be perfect and gives us room to learn and grow.

So when I suggest that you take your pencil, pen, art materials, and journal outdoors with you, I don't want you to get all panicky on me. This is NOT an exercise in how good you are, how well you can write, or how beautifully you can draw. This is an exercise in finding ways to express what nature reveals to you. As you will see throughout this book, the poems and stories from myself and other contributors are spontaneous expressions, shared from pages of our journals or personal conversations. This is a chance for you to express what you see and feel without reservation. No one will be grading your essay or critiquing your artwork.

The second thing we need to talk about is your brain. Scientists tell us that we use only 13 percent of our brains most of the time. This neocortex portion of the brain, called the new brain, has only two functions: language and reason. We have cultivated the new brain to translate the old brain senses into words and logic, which is essential for our living, but the problem is,

Nature often holds up a mirror so we can see more clearly the ongoing processes of growth, renewal, and transformation in our lives.

—MARY ANN BRUSSAT

23

language and reason take us away from direct experience, making it secondhand.

The difference between a secondhand experience and a direct experience is a little like the difference between drawing a stereotypical leaf shape from memory (most of us would draw something in basic green, with little personality) versus taking a walk on a late autumn day through a forest rich with the color of changing leaves and really seeing the wide variety of shapes and textures. When our new brains translate an experience and stamp it with a generic shape and color, we are robbed of truly seeing.

But when we tap into the other 87 percent of the brain—the old brain—we move into the arena of senses and feelings. These uninterpreted emotions provide a direct link to our core self. In small children the new brain is not yet fully developed, so they are much more oriented to sensate experiences. Think about it for a moment. Do you remember, or can you imagine, those endless days of summer in childhood that you spent playing in the sandbox, sifting grains of sand through your fingers, and loving the gritty texture? Adding water to make a moat for your castle? Your mother calling and calling to get your attention? Even if it was lunch time, you were not hungry because the moment was so full.

That is the kind of openness I am talking about: being present to every one of your senses so you can be in the moment. I like the way Philip Chard, a psychotherapist who uses nature in his work, puts it:

[To] come back to the senses, back to the language of the Earth ... is easier said than satisfied, especially for those of us who make our livings by thinking, planning, and worrying, but it can be done. Just visit home. Nature is still there. It will call you in. All you need to do is listen, smell, taste, see, and touch. Thinking is unnecessary and distracting.

This is the invitation nature extends to you: "Just visit home ... listen, smell, taste, see, and touch." You can come back to yourself by coming back to your senses, by being aware of your physical sensations and your emotions, by being present to whatever nature reveals to you.

Are you ready?

Upon entering wilderness, one of the first things almost everyone experiences is an enlivening of the five senses.... This awakening of our senses, or perhaps better stated, "coming to our senses," is a subtly powerful and underrated experience.

—STEVEN HARPER,
ECOPSYCHOLOGY

An Awakening Experience

If you were to come to a SPA Sisters Awakening Retreat, this exercise would be one of your first experiences. But, fortunately, this experience isn't limited to a particular place or group of people. The outdoor spot you choose can be anywhere you live. Think of a patch of nature that you can get to without a lot of hassle. It could be a local park or forest preserve, your neighborhood, or even your own backyard.

Give yourself an hour or so to be silent in an outdoor spot of your choice. (If you are doing this with another person or group, be sure to agree on a specific period of silence.) Bring with you a journal, a pen or pencil, and, if you wish, art supplies; these will be the tools you use to reflect on your experience.

The main thing to bring with you is your awareness. What attracts you in the natural setting? What are you drawn to? Listen to your interior to notice what catches your attention. As you set out, keep this question in mind:

> • What in nature do I see as precious or
> valuable?

Once you get to your patch of nature, it's time to let go. Start walking slowly. Leave the day's agenda behind. Let go of any expectations of how you "should" do this exercise. Become

With practice and patience, sensory awareness can be cultivated to a more focused awareness I call "attentiveness." In wilderness, we begin to develop a sustained continuum of mindfulness.

—STEVEN HARPER,
ECOPSYCHOLOGY

aware of your breathing in and out. Smell the day. Look up and down and around. Listen to the sounds. Close your eyes and notice which sounds are more acute or which sounds emerge. When you open your eyes, if you notice a texture that you want to touch, go ahead. Close your eyes again as you feel and focus on the texture. Let your mind wander. Be aware of any attraction you might have to any sight or sound or smell.

When you notice something that calls to you, find a place where you can sit and reflect on it with these questions:

- What caught my attention?

- What seems precious or valuable about this particular element of nature?

- What does my attraction to this say about me?

Allow yourself to be in the moment, to be aware of all your senses. As thoughts and feelings come to you, use your journal to record them. You might want to write a free-floating association or "scribble draw." I find it helpful to use the form of haiku to help me focus on the essence of the experience. A haiku has only three lines, with a simple structure of five syllables in the first line, seven in the second, and five in the last. Though I am almost never able to stay perfectly in those parameters, I find haiku a great way to stay in the present.

When you take a flower in your hand and really look at it, it's your world for the moment.
—GEORGIA O'KEEFFE

However you respond to the questions, be gentle with yourself. Linger where and when you want. Get up and walk some more. Write or draw, hum or laugh, dance or weep—whatever reflects your experience of the moment.

If you are undertaking this retreat with others, when you come back together, give each woman ample time to disclose whatever she wishes to share. It is good to have one person loosely leading the group to ensure that all have time to be heard. The main task for the group is to tune in and really listen to each person and enjoy her presence. If a person would like a response, share out of your own experience (preferably a nature experience). Remember that each of us has our own answers, and our role is to be patient with each other as we unearth them. We do not need to judge, give advice, or fix anyone. When everyone has finished, you might want to take time to gather in a circle and name the things you are grateful for that have come out of this time together.

If you are undertaking these experiences one week at a time, use the following activity for the time in between: Spend intentional time outside and allow yourself to soak in your own value as part of nature's glorious dance. Journal about your feelings. If you are participating in this exploration with others, share some of your thoughts and feelings at the start of your next meeting.

TWO
Grounding
RESTORING YOUR ROOTS

Herons and the Kingdom of Heaven

I want to introduce you to Harry. Harry is a great blue heron whom I've taken the liberty of naming. I see him occasionally when we are on Dauphin Island in the Gulf of Mexico, and every time I catch a glimpse of him, he inspires me. As be bends his knee and lifts his leg, high strutting his next step, he has an unflappable presence. Sometimes he tucks one leg up into his fluffy self as he nods off for his afternoon snooze. He obviously has no care for what I think of him as he lives his life ... unless I invade his space! I learn a lot about living life from Harry.

Harry blue heron
Here there and everywhere
On his island home
Stretching neck straight up

Body upright, wings out warming
Total comfort ... healthy narcissism
Unafraid, unabashed.
I want to be like you, Harry!

Harry reminds me of my earliest child self and my desire for that young, fresh self to be fully part of me now. I see my earliest self as God's creation, untarnished by the broken world as yet, brimming unabashedly with vitality. I'm reminded of something Jesus said when his disciples asked him who was the greatest in the kingdom of heaven. He responded, "I tell you the truth, unless you change and become like little children, you will never enter the kingdom of heaven. Therefore, whoever humbles [herself] like this child is the greatest in the kingdom of heaven" (Matthew 18:3–4 NIV).

For most of us, our child self is a dim memory, and we are consumed by busy lives with little time or energy for childhood whimsies. That little girl who used to go out and play is but a fantasy, and truth be told, we might even feel a little embarrassed if she were to pop up now without warning. But that child self is the part of us that knows the pure joy of making snow angels, building sand castles, or watching fireflies. As adults, we've set aside our willingness to be immersed in our senses and in imaginative activities to make way for more pressing needs. We've been lured by any number of things and activities and expectations, and are working so hard to pay for it all that we end up

We could never have loved the earth so well if we had had no childhood in it.

—WILLA CATHER

30

feeling stressed or empty, without understanding why. We sense that we have lost something important and, at times, make attempts to recapture it by scheduling a day or a weekend—a week, if we're lucky—for an escape, if we can squeeze it in.

I vote for restoration, not escape!

Recently, I accompanied a friend who was going to purchase a TV at one of the big-box chain stores. The store sat in a huge shopping center that appeared to be made entirely of concrete. The giant parking lot was jammed, and hundreds of people were heading in and out of the store in a steady stream. I certainly had never seen a forest preserve so crowded! The inside was windowless, with banks of cold light overhead. I felt claustrophobic and drained even before I reached the TV aisle. Wasn't this supposed to be fun? The whole experience was exhausting and in no way rejuvenating.

I live near a large thoroughfare grandly called the Randall Road Corridor. Doesn't that sound ominous? When I drive the full length of it, the same megastores repeat every five or ten miles. If I did not pay attention, I could easily forget where I am. To put it bluntly, we are in danger of not only forgetting *where* we are, but *who* we are. Along the way of progress, we have lost ourselves, our authentic core, the part of us that knows who we are and what our purpose is. We have lost our grounding—literally. As a psychotherapist, I see how this has induced an epidemic sense of emptiness rather than abundance. No TV set—not even the best high-definition screen we can find—can tell us who we are. Many of us have settled for virtual lives. Often, we read about living or we watch someone else living on TV, or we talk about living (usually about how hard it is, how awful the world is, and how busy we are), but we don't actually live the life we were created to live.

When my husband, Leon, and I first moved to Prairie Lake, we extended an open invitation to our neighbor to fish in our lake anytime he wanted to. He never came.

One day, Leon dropped by to visit the man and found him playing a virtual fishing game on his computer. He said that's how he liked to fish!

Like that neighbor, we are all moving further and further from what is real. As a culture, we have upgraded ourselves with technology that keeps us electronically connected, but we have lessened our connection with our selves and with nature. We have turned away from what is most authentic, from our deepest core, and we need to find our roots again.

Deep Roots

If I were to look directly into your eyes and tell you that I see a passionate, unique, creative human being, you might not recognize yourself. This description is probably not the first thing you think of when you wake up in the morning. But the truth is, this is who you were created to be. One of my favorite psalms is a celebration of praise for The Artist's intention:

> *You are the one*
> *who put me together*
> *inside my mother's body,*
> *and I praise you*
> *because of*
> *the wonderful way*
> *you created me.*
> *Everything you do is marvelous!*
> *Of this I have no doubt.*
> *Nothing about me*

Is hidden from you!
I was secretly woven together
deep in the earth below,
but with your own eyes
you saw
my body being formed. (Psalm 139:13–16 CEV)

Your spirit, your innermost being, the part of you that is alive and feeling and connected to something larger, is the essence your authentic self. *Webster's* defines *authentic* as "not false or imitation; real, actual." If you want to reconnect with the authentic person you are at your core, you can find her again. It's a matter of getting back to your roots.

The midwestern prairies have much to teach us about the importance of roots. The root system of the compass plant, for example, is vast and complex. These remarkable plants not only grow up to twelve feet tall, but their branchlike "trunks" and roots also grow down, as mentioned earlier, an amazing fifteen feet below the surface. When the early settlers first arrived on the prairie, they found these giants among a jungle tangle that must have been incredibly difficult to move through. By the time the steel plow finally got the land under human control, the original prairie had become unrecognizable. It was now disguised as vast fields of soybeans and corn that sucked up the nutrients of the rich black soil created by the prairie ecosystem.

I am fully committed to the idea that human existence should be rooted in the earth.

—CARL JUNG

Does any of this resonate with you? Think about it: The Artist of Creation formed us to bloom in beauty, but we are being sucked dry of nutrients by the very culture we have built to get our lives under control. Back in the fifties, the first ads that celebrated automatic washers and dryers featured women in poofy housedresses, undergirded by cancan slips, dancing around their new appliances. These ads promised "time-saving conveniences" that would lead to a twenty-five-hour work week by the nineties. What that promise did not take into account was that, as we created more and more stuff—expensive stuff!—we would need to work more and more hours to afford it. Perhaps getting control is a poor substitute for restoring beauty.

In Illinois, where I live, there used to be more than twenty-two million acres of native prairie, but now only some two thousand acres of the original prairie are left. There are a few places that haven't ever been plowed under, a few pockets where prairie remnants remain—mostly where we hadn't been able to plant anything else, such as along the edges of old railroad tracks. As people realized that we had nearly destroyed the prairie ecosystem, new pioneers of the late twentieth century started collecting seeds from these remnants while researching what would help them germinate. Prairie restoration projects began to pop up little by little, as people began the slow process of reseeding and nurturing the land back to its original ecosystem. Gradually, as concerned individuals recognize the beauty of this ecosystem, the prairie is being restored. It is coming back

Everybody needs beauty as well as bread, places to stay in and places to pray in, where nature may heal and give strength to body and soul alike.

—JOHN MUIR

even in unlikely places. For example, in the middle of Millennium Park in downtown Chicago, a section of recreated prairie landscape reminds and inspires people of the natural beauty we almost lost.

When we first moved to Prairie Lake, it surely didn't look as though it had ever been a prairie. I decided to plant native seeds partly because prairie restoration seemed like a noble cause, and partly because I couldn't think of what else we could do with the nine acres where the soybeans and corn used to reside. A notable thing happened in the process: as the prairie was gradually restored, so was I.

I spent hundreds of hours walking in, working in, sitting in, reading in, and painting the prairie, and I experienced a sense of solitude literally baking into my being. I had forgotten the power of quiet, the invigorating energy of wind, the joy of newly sprouted seeds. And I began to learn patience. Though the foot-tall black-eyed Susans came back that first year, it took a number of years for the majestic, deep-rooted compass plant to take hold. As the prairie and I grew together, the compass plants taught me an important lesson: Neither fire nor wind nor drought nor hot sun can destroy these tough plants. They die only when they are uprooted from their soil. As long as their root system is intact, they continue to grow.

Consider for a minute the significance of this prairie metaphor. I believe that, as people created by The Artist who formed both the vastness of the universe and the tiniest seed, we

How does the Meadow flower its bloom unfold? Because the lovely little flower is free down to its root, and in that freedom bold.

—William Wordsworth

are deeply rooted in God. When we are rooted in our true selves and our Creator, our spirit lives. Even when we're blown and burned by life's storms, our deep roots patiently wait for us to tend them back to life. Our challenge as "cultivated" human beings is the sacred task of finding these remnants of self to work with and restore.

Nature School

One October I looked out from the house at what appeared to be my carefully tended, emerald-green front lawn. However, when I went out on the porch and looked more closely, I noticed that the landscaping at the front of the house was being invaded by the grass trying to take over the ground cover. And it looked as if the grass was succeeding. Even though I work at keeping them separate, plants have another way of being. Even though I work at making them appear tame, they are wild. Even though I have lived in the structure of humankind many years and probably appear well-coifed, I, too, am wild at the core. I am part of nature.

That's good news for me—and for you. Because we all started out connected with nature, we can go back to nature to find our true selves. I first noticed this connection when I began intentionally going outside to walk or, even better, sit quietly. I found myself noticing the sky's color and how the clouds were formed. When I took time to watch the flow of the river, I saw how the sparkly light hit the rougher currents, while the smoother sur-

I came to see myself as growing out of the earth like the other native animals and plants. I saw my body and my daily motions as brief coherences and articulations of the energy of the place, which would fall back into it like leaves in the autumn.

—WENDELL BERRY

faces looked like glassy reflections. As I sat quietly, animals, ducks, and geese started dropping by my bench, coming remarkably closer, appearing to be tame, willing to merge their lives with mine for a moment.

Remember the March retreat I described in the first chapter, the one with the nasty weather? That same afternoon, after lunch in my cozy office, I returned to the wild day outside. My journal entry starts:

Wind blowing,
River running,
Ducks paddle in the safety of the bay.
   I need to remember there is always a safe harbor. Thank you,
God. I notice the swiftly moving river beelining into a quieter
bay. I am like the swiftly moving river much of the time.
I wonder how it would feel if I beelined into the bay.
   I find a place nestled into the rock steps and sit. As I stop,
two geese move closer ... now maybe eight feet away. We are really in this
together ... in community. Another goose is floating over to me on the bay ...
now three feet away. I can see his little webbed feet kicking under the water.
Goose preening
Neck and head curved back
Beak poking pruning
A show I would have missed if I hadn't waited.
Maybe I need to slow down so life can come to me ...

In those quiet moments of reflection, nature showed me something about my core self, something that brought me back to center. Or perhaps more accurately, I gave a meaning to what I saw in nature based on who I am. Either way, nature was my teacher. This is not a new idea, but a homecoming to an old truth. In the Hebrew Bible's book of Job, this ancient truth resounds in the words, "Speak to the earth and it will teach you" (Job 12:8 NIV).

Nature school offers a wide variety of learning and rich metaphors for living. Metaphors from nature can mirror our experiences and offer ways to better understand ourselves and what we are going through. For example, many have reflected on ways the changing seasons represent life cycles: the fullness of summer followed by a sense of loss in the fall; grief in the barrenness of winter followed by the renewal of hope with the coming spring. Nature's symbols also have meanings for us that are uniquely personal. When we intentionally go outside with an attitude of openness to what we might learn, and pay attention to what we are attracted to, nature can reflect back to us a wealth of information about who we are at our core.

Even as I write this, describing how important it is to actually *go outside,* I realize that I am sitting indoors looking out at a quiet, white blanket of snow. It's the first snowfall of the season, and I find myself thinking about the crisp, cold air. I notice that the Japanese maple leaves are still clinging to the tree. Suddenly, I nudge myself with a laugh: "Here you are *thinking* about the outdoors, suggesting that *other* people go outdoors ... what are you waiting for?"

You will find something far greater in the woods than you will find in books. Stones and trees will teach you that which you will never learn from masters.

—Saint Bernard of Clairvaux

So I pile on my boots, hat, and jacket and head outside. It is only then that I feel the cold and am struck by the quiet. Only out here can I hear the sound of birds chirping. Then I notice my neighbor Bob refilling his myriad bird feeders. I think about ignoring him, but instead yell, "Hi, Bob." I proceed to tell him I am writing a book about nature, and he gestures to the woods behind our houses, as though that were the only place to find nature.

We laugh, but I head in another direction. As I move on, I notice the refreshing, icy air in my nostrils. Suddenly, I hear honking geese above and am riveted when I look up. Flying overhead are hundreds of geese in a huge V shape. What really attracts me, however, are five or six stragglers in the middle of the V. They are not in formation and are instead weaving in and out. Gradually, they reenter the V, but then some others seem to break out of the rigid lines of formation to become a new set of stragglers. This observation seems important to me. As I walk back to my house, Bob pops up and announces he loves the cold: "It's so crisp and clean." We laugh again and I go back inside.

What does all this mean to me? First, I rarely talk to Bob, who is, after all, part of nature. Today I learned that he loves the cold winter air and that he likes to take a minute to laugh with a neighbor. It is a moment of presence. I think I will take more time for a "Hi, Bob."

And what about the V? I know that this formation is an efficient, functional one that allows each bird to take advantage of the lift power of the bird in

Our blueprint shows that our natural senses are an intelligent continuum that only exist in each immediate moment. We either make time and space to become conscious of our natural senses in the moment or we miss out on their wisdom.

—MICHAEL COHEN,
RECONNECTING WITH
NATURE

Look deep into nature, and then you will understand everything better.

—ALBERT EINSTEIN

front of it, and that the birds fall back out of the lead position when they get tired. But on this particular day, I saw it differently. I thought about how I can easily become a V person, staying in formation, going on doing what I think I must. Maybe my attraction to the stragglers who broke formation is a hint about part of me that wants out of the V, that wants a broader, richer life ... a Sabbath from the need to press forward.

When I return to my cozy indoor nest, I feel thankful and a bit wiser. My prayer goes something like this: "Thank you, God. Help me to be a straggler more often."

It was a rich way to spend ten minutes.

Metaphors-in-Waiting

In my life as a psychotherapist, I've attended many classes and seminars (and there have been *many*!) that were based on the model of "input, input, input." In other words, someone else telling me something, giving me information. The first time I designed a retreat, I tried to pare down my input, but I still had a lot to say. Then a wonderful thing happened: as I listened to people's stories, I began to recognize that each of us has a rich vein of wisdom running through our being, and what we need is spacious time and a safe place to access it.

As I explored this idea more deeply in my retreats and with friends, I began to realize that something amazing was happening: when we went outside to harvest our own metaphors, we

Sometimes, if you stand on the bottom rail of a bridge and lean over to watch the river slipping slowly away beneath you, you will suddenly know everything there is to be known.

—WINNIE THE POOH

could count on our creative processes to help us to recognize what we needed to know. This apparently simple premise has layer upon layer of form and meaning. It is rich and deep, like getting to the crystalline center of a geode. I eventually realized that, instead of the "here's what I want to tell you" approach, the "what do you see, taste, touch, smell, feel" approach gets past our carefully constructed, tough stone exterior and into our center where things become clear and focused.

Susan Scott, a therapist from Arizona, describes a similar phenomenon that took place in her practice. Because she had back trouble and could no longer sit comfortably, she started walking outside with her clients. Once outdoors, she was amazed to find that not only were her clients growing through the rich metaphors in nature, but so was she: "I was so surprised to recognize how my worry had transformed to prayer with the inspiration of nature's language."

In the women's classic *Gift from the Sea,* Anne Morrow Lindbergh offered a beautiful range of shell metaphors that were important to her understanding of life. Though her book was published in 1955—an era that now seems serenely quiet compared to today's whirl of technology and harried pace—Lindbergh already had a sense that the world's pulse was picking up. When she returned from a trip to a quiet beach, she wrote:

> I can only carry back my little channeled whelk. It will sit on my desk in Connecticut, to remind me of the ideal of a simplified life, to encourage me in the game I played on the beach, to ask how little, not how much, can I get along with. To say—is it necessary?—when I am tempted to add one more accumulation to my life, when I am pulled toward one more centrifugal activity.

Lindbergh reminds us that metaphors from nature can help us remember what's important. As we meditate, write, make music, draw pictures, or create dances about these images, we can continue to unearth their meanings for our lives.

One of the gifts of nature's metaphors is that they are always available, waiting to bring us home to our roots. And one of the reassurances we have is that we already have the skill set needed to find them. There's only thing we need to do: pay attention.

When you step out into nature, you need only be open to what attracts you, what catches your interest. It is not necessary to figure out the "why" of the attraction while you are experiencing it; simply notice the symbols and metaphors that speak to you. Later, as you take time to reflect on those symbols and metaphors, core truths about yourself will emerge that can be useful for self-discovery and understanding, whether you are in a time of abundance or are experiencing loss, depression, or stress in your life.

Another benefit of attending nature school is that it doesn't cost money or require complicated preparations. You can step into a full-of-wonder way by simply stopping what you are doing and stepping outside. You already have what you need; no equipment is necessary (except, perhaps, a jacket and your journal). There is no pressure; when you're outdoors, you do not have to do it all. If you take the time to slow down, look, and listen, treasures *will* show up on your path.

Learning to attend is the first step in developing an ecological way of seeing. Attending is the flip side of psychic numbing; it is the enhancement of selected sensory information.

—LAURA SEWALL,
ECOPSYCHOLOGY

Companions on the Journey

As a therapist, I have heard untold numbers of women's stories, and I have found that every woman's story is like her fingerprints—completely individual. As we listen to the stories of our companions on the journey, we can find hints of restorable remnants within ourselves. I hope you have a chance to share your stories with other women. I've asked a few of my SPA Sisters if I could share their stories with you in the pages of this book. As you read them, listen carefully for the elements in their stories that resonate with you.

My friend Eileen's story has roots in the sunny flats of the Midwest, but she followed her innate desire for adventure and creative vision in her move to the East Coast. As we talked, she related some of the meanings the metaphor of a river has for her:

> *I live on the Hudson River. I love water. Water is like dancing; it's always moving. So whether it's foggy or there are lots of waves or the sun reflects differently, it's dynamically different every day. I would like to think that I, too, am dynamically different every day. I don't know if that's true, but I do know that I get bored easily and that I thrive on change.*
>
> *Spiritually, I guess this says I like to be alive and fluid, moving with whatever's happening and going with the flow. My river metaphor expresses the*

Wise, appropriated stories tell us to choose to reconnect with nature, enjoy it, and grow from it. When we heed these stories, our stress wanes and relationships improve.

—MICHAEL COHEN,
RECONNECTING WITH
NATURE

changes in my life and self. It's about swimming with the river, rather than just going with the flow. It's actively engaging, putting myself on the right "path."

For a long time in my business, I was going with the flow, with what somebody needed, with the phone call that came in, with the meeting where I was expected, rather than consciously making choices about where I wanted to put my spirit. And then I got to a place where I was feeling tossed around by the waves rather than actively engaged in swimming in the river. For me, the metaphor of the river is about making choices but still being open to the flow, to the spirit part of it.

I think, too, of Deb, whom you met in the last chapter. In the afternoon of her SPA Sisters Awakening Retreat, I asked each woman, as I always do, to go out into nature and find a metaphor that reflected who they wanted to become. You might remember Deb's story of finding a duck who somehow managed to keep balanced on a slippery rock. She also noticed a turtle sunning itself on another exposed rock. As she thought about her mission in life as a therapist, about her work of helping others come out of their "shell," she wrote in her journal:

LESSONS FROM THE TURTLE

Sunning on a rock
The turtle signals to me
Come and be with me.

Look at the turtle.
She wears her house on her back.
"Simplify" she says.

I am called to simplify. Can I be like the turtle with my belongings on my back? Soon I will need to transition into a simpler way of living. Can I trust and let go of what I love and make room for the new and different? The turtle tells me I am called to crawl out of the fast flowing river and experience a different slower current,

to rest and warm myself in the sun-
to soak in the silence,
to be.

Since her diagnosis of cancer in 1995 and again in 2001, Deb has returned to nature as an important part of her healing: "My love affair with nature has been an ongoing process since I was a child. Gardening is a 'soul activity' where I experience no sense of time. Slowly, I have begun to see metaphors in nature that teach me about life, death, myself, and God."

Another friend, Gail Castle, described her Awakening Retreat experience like this: "Taking part in the retreat was a surprise awakening to my connection with nature. Although I have always preferred to be outside rather than inside, this retreat allowed me to stop and observe and reflect on what calls me out of my living room, through the screen door, and onto the green carpet of nature." The metaphor Gail found for herself that day was a spider in her web:

The silence of the Plains, this great unpeopled landscape of earth and sky, is much like the silence one finds in a monastery, an unfathomable silence that has the power to re-form you.

—KATHLEEN NORRIS

I stop to observe the spider in her web. She is delicate—the finest of features, most flexible of limbs. Yet she is able to build the strongest of webs and use it for the immediate purpose, waiting patiently for results. Many things will ultimately destroy her work. But she is never flustered. She carries on with tenacity. Sometimes she builds in open areas and sometimes in shelters, always with the understanding that this web is temporary and that her ability to weave it is a gift that she uses with passion. She wastes no time in realms outside her passion. I take my lesson from her. I want to become passionate, useful, tenacious, and content with the gifts I have been given.

You might be interested to know that since her retreat experience, Gail has chosen to tenaciously pursue a graduate degree in psychology.

At a SPA Sisters Awakening Retreat, we do have a marvelous time, and being with other women is definitely a supportive plus of the experience, but it's not necessary to travel to any specific program or retreat to find nature images that speak to you. I'm going to walk you through the afternoon exercise of an Awakening Retreat so you can experience the power of nature's metaphors for yourself, in your own backyard or neighborhood, in a park or woods. If you have been ignoring parts of yourself lately—or have a sense that some part of you has gotten lost somewhere, or that you have been masking some part of your true self because of shame or rejection—you can begin your personal restoration project today by reconnecting with nature.

Before you start this exercise, notice that I used the word *begin*. Restoration is a lifelong process; you will always be in the process of becoming. In our goal-oriented culture, that probably doesn't sound particularly attractive. Frankly, I like that I will never be *there,* wherever *there* might be. Normally, I want to make things happen. But when I let myself trust that restoration is an ongoing process of learning and growing, and I choose to cooperate with this process, I can relax. What a relief it is not to have to finish everything in order to move on!

Are you ready to reclaim your original beauty? Are you ready to discover the remnants of your child self that remain? In order to know *where* you want to go, you need first to be conscious of *who* you are. Remember: Nature is waiting to reveal herself— and you. All you need to do is be attentive to the moment.

In the process of growth and transformation we must begin to reclaim and own the rejected parts of ourselves. The essence of wilderness practice is to be wilderness.

—STEVEN HARPER,
ECOPSYCHOLOGY

Come forth into the light of things. Let Nature be your teacher.

—WILLIAM WORDSWORTH

A Grounding Experience

Give yourself an hour or so to be silent in an outdoor spot of your choice. Dress so that you will be comfortable outside and bring your journal, pens, pencils, and art materials. (Remember, these are tools for expression, not perfection! I'll tell you a little story that might help: I recently heard that a fancy new camera was used to photograph the *Mona Lisa,* and it revealed many layers of paint-overs and changes. If you have a little perfectionist voice inside, tell her you need a little time to explore and that it is going to be okay.)

As you move into the natural place you have chosen, slowly quiet yourself and allow your awareness of the environment to become more conscious. (If you are undertaking this retreat with others, you may chat on your way, but when you get to your space, please be silent for the time you spend there so you can be fully present to what nature might reveal to you.)

Let yourself relax into openness. Be aware of what attracts you, of what nature might be reflecting to you about who you are. As you walk about in your chosen place, check in with your senses. What are the fragrances you smell? Close your eyes to hear the sounds so you can distinguish them more clearly. As you open your eyes, allow yourself to take in this natural setting, inspecting it as though you have never seen it before. Be aware of what is going on inside of you, of what might be calling to you. Look around with this question in mind:

- Where does my attention rest?

Allow yourself to stay focused on what interests you, and consider these two questions:

- How might this be a metaphor for who I am?

- How might it be a metaphor for who I want to become?

You might find that you need two different metaphors to answer these questions. That's fine. You may want to spend more time on the first question before you can move on to the second. You might want to split these questions into two different nature experiences, in order to give yourself the time you need with each.

When you have chosen your nature attraction (or it has chosen you), find a spot where you can settle and write in your journal about your feelings, senses, and responses to the two questions. Draw symbols or colors or pictures that represent what you are experiencing. Or perhaps you'd like to focus on the moment with a haiku or poem.

Then let your mind consider one more possibility:

- Is there one small step I can take sometime soon to bring my vision for who I want to become into being?

Nobody sees a flower, really—it is so small— we haven't time, and to see takes time, like to have a friend takes time.

—Georgia O'Keeffe

After you have jotted down a possibility, set your journal and materials aside and let your body respond to this idea. Allow your body to move and see how it feels. You can also reflect further on your experience through meditation (just being in the moment, aware of your senses), art, journal writing, or poetry, whatever form of expression that allows you to be yourself. Take the time to see, hear, and feel who you are. Allow your experience to simmer in your mind and heart and jot down any continued learnings and ideas.

If you are undertaking this retreat with others, gather in a circle when you come back together and give each other time to share what has been important about this experience. Remember, when another woman is speaking, your role is to listen attentively and *really* hear her ... and enjoy her. If she says that she desires your response, share only out of your own experience, with no attempt to give advice or fix her. She will come to her own answers. When everyone has finished, you might want to take time to name the things you are grateful for that have come out of this time together.

If you are undertaking these experiences one week at a time, use the following activity for the time in between: Spend time outside and allow yourself to dream about possibilities for your life as you meander. Be aware of what you are drawn to in nature. Journal about your ideas. If you are participating in this exploration with others, bring your ideas to share at the start of your next meeting.

THREE
Energizing

EXPERIENCING YOUR CLEAR, FLOWING WELLSPRING

Children Have It

Do you remember ever feeling like this?

When the screen door flew open, my little legs raced me across the lawn to adventures unknown. When asked what I did outside, my response was usually, "Nothing." Ohhh, but how exquisite that nothing was! My heart just wanted my toes to tangle in the cool grass. My eyes coveted glances at the shimmer of the belly of a Japanese beetle or a fly eye. My body desired to feel the delicious, dizzying effect of staring at the clouds. I sensed the world spin as I lay flat on the ground, looking up at a world of clouds whizzing by with a gentle wave to me. My nose

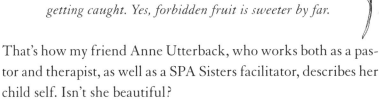

As a child, one has that magical capacity ... to see the land as an animal does; to experience the sky from the perspective of a flower or a bee; to feel the earth quiver and breathe beneath us.

—VALERIE ANDREWS,
A PASSION FOR THIS EARTH

At birth we are biologically at one with nature. We are born illiterate because nature is a nonverbal way of knowing and being.

—MICHAEL COHEN,
*RECONNECTING
WITH NATURE*

sniffled out the exotic fragrances of musty mushrooms and gardenias. My tongue touched the tender shoots of nectar found on honeysuckle stems. I sought the crunchy fresh chomp of a green apple— which resulted in more than one problem with the farmer who owned the tree next to the school playground. There is nothing like eating a warm fresh apple as you sit in the fork of a branch, tickled by the leaves, while your spirit is titillated by the prospect of getting caught. Yes, forbidden fruit is sweeter by far.

That's how my friend Anne Utterback, who works both as a pastor and therapist, as well as a SPA Sisters facilitator, describes her child self. Isn't she beautiful?

Each of us starts out with this instinctive draw to the natural world, this kind of sensual awareness, this pure delight in the world and ourselves. In SPA Sisters we use the metaphor of a wellspring to describe this free-flowing life energy that we are born with. Just as a wellspring in nature is the source for the continuous flow of a stream, so, too, is our inner wellspring an abundant source of creativity, hope, playfulness, love, and happiness. As children, we could keep our wellsprings full and naturally cared for by playing and spending time in nature. We could relish everything the outdoors had to offer: climbing trees, collecting sticks and rocks, feeling cool breezes, running barefoot in the grass, and splashing in puddles.

I have a memory of myself wearing a yellow dotted-swiss dress, standing on a vibrantly green, grassy hill. As soon as this picture comes to mind, I can almost *feel* that breezy day. I remember how intensely blue the sky was, and how white and puffy the clouds were. As I visualize my full skirt billowing in the wind, looking almost transparent, I still have a sense of my child delight. In that memory moment, I know what it is like to feel pretty, expectant, and full of hope.

Many of us, somewhere along the way, have stopped experiencing this kind of spontaneous adventure and excitement. As adults, our wellsprings have become clouded or blocked—even dried up. Our lives are filled with the responsibilities of work, family, and bills, and we spend much of our time indoors, with scarce time for fun, creativity, or connection to nature. We have lost sight of that little girl who used to go out and play, who did not worry about trying to impress others or justify her worth.

Nature therapist Philip Chard has written a poignant lament about this lost treasure:

> Before we brainwash children with the mistaken notion that they are not offspring of the Earth, they revel in the natural world, undaunted by rain, snow, mud, grass stains, wind and cold lakes; all the experiences their parents seek to protect them from. Before long, many of them learn from the adults in their midst that getting wet, dirty, ruffled, sweaty, or

Somehow the great clouds made the day all right, a gift of splendor as they sailed over our heads.

—MAY SARTON

otherwise imprinted by the Earth is to be discouraged and, if necessary, corrected.

Perhaps as you're reading this, you're mentally arguing, "But I had a *lousy* childhood." If I were to tell you what went on in my house growing up, you would probably agree that I did as well. But I have found that, when I carefully look back, I can see moments of life and light. Even the clients with whom I've worked in drug rehab, who have had mostly disastrous childhood experiences, often found they could uncover some light from that time. It is my premise that if we can re-access our sensory childhood experiences in nature, we can find the path back to our authentic selves.

The Eighth Level of Intelligence

When the first pioneers in covered wagons laid eyes on the midwestern prairie, they were confronted by something most of them had probably never seen before: a seemingly unending sea of tall grass. Listen to the way John Madson describes it in *Where the Sky Began: Land of the Tallgrass Prairie:*

> It was flowing emerald in spring and summer when
> the boundless winds ran across it, a tawny ocean under
> the winds of autumn.... Each stem of prairie grass
> stands straight, a slender antenna between the flood of

Now, my tree-climbing days long behind me, I often think about the lasting value of those early, deliciously idle days. I have come to appreciate the long view afforded by those treetops.

—RICHARD LOUV,
LAST CHILD IN THE WOODS

solar energy and the deep banks of stored energy within the soil. Unlike the miserly trees, a grass does not hoard that energy by tying it up in woody structure. The grass spends itself freely and annually, deepening and fattening the black soils below and pouring strength into the animal biomass above.

I believe a leaf of grass is no less than the journey-work of the stars.
—WALT WHITMAN

Can you picture this? Even though only remnants of the virgin prairie remain, Madson's sensual words give a hint of the life force of this wild land before it was cultivated.

When Leon and I began restoring the prairie at Prairie Lake, I had little idea how beautiful *grass* could be! We started by planting nine acres with native Illinois prairie seeds, and by the third year I was up to my nose in grasses. Big bluestem, also known as turkey foot, the dominant species of tall prairie grass, occasionally grows up to nine feet high and makes a beautiful contrast with the rusty, feathery spires of Indian grass that wave in the wind. When I walk the land, wave upon wave of tall prairie grass sways back and forth with the breeze, and I feel like a small child surrounded by giants. Talk about a way to reconnect with my inner child!

Over the years, I have facilitated many inner-child groups, and one thing I've consistently observed is that the bonds that develop between participants are nothing short of extraordinary. It is my hunch that they happen because they become "childhood" friends. Do you remember the easy closeness of this kind of bond? I remember my early friend Sherry Stiles. We would beat a path to each other's home and play all day, till dark—mostly outside, of course. I would eat at her house and she at mine. It was simple and seamless. I felt crushed for her when she wore her Halloween costume to school on the wrong day! We were there for one another in a very natural way. When I was eight, my family moved, and I still wonder where she is. (Please get in touch with me if you read this, Sherry!) These deep bonds of childhood, these connections that we once had to people, to animals and nature, and to our unadorned selves, are full of life, energy, playfulness, hope, and happiness that I believe we can re-access.

One hot summer day I was leading a retreat out on the prairie, and I nestled down in the thick of it for some quiet moments. Out of the grasses, two speckled fawns emerged, dancing by. They almost missed noticing me until we were practically nose-to-nose. One ran off to find Mom, but the other stayed about five feet away and hid behind a lacy yellow coneflower plant for several minutes. It was not a very successful disguise, but it was a compelling image. It made me think of childlike trust and vulnerability. As adults, I think it is possible to keep our adult wisdom and discernment but also retrieve the wonder-filled and wilder qualities we had as children.

Even though I've used nature as an avenue to the true self in my work as a therapist and retreat leader for over

Forget not that the earth delights to feel your bare feet and the winds long to play with your hair.

—Kahlil Gibran

twenty years, I keep discovering more and more gifts from the natural world. Did you know research has shown that people who participate in "nature reconnecting methods and materials" experience "measurable benefits"? Michael Cohen elaborates in his book *Reconnecting with Nature:*

> Environmental literacy, citizenship, and learning ability rise.
> Participation reduces apathy, abuse of people, substance abuse, depression, sleeplessness and loneliness. We enjoy educational, environmental, aesthetic, and economic benefits. Our spirit, energy, and self-esteem soar.

I've been fascinated by the work of Howard Gardner, a Harvard University psychologist who has delineated multiple kinds of intelligence. For instance, when we see a mime, we have a certain fascination with his or her bodily or kinesthetic ability, which is outside the framework we ordinarily think of as intelligence. Gardner named seven kinds of intelligence in his 1983 book *Frames of Mind: The Theory of Multiple Intelligences:* linguistic intelligence, logical-mathematical intelligence, spatial intelligence, bodily-kinesthetic intelligence, musical intelligence, interpersonal intelligence, and intrapersonal intelligence.

But here's the fun part: in 1996, Gardner added an eighth intelligence—naturalist intelligence—which involves how we relate information to our natural surroundings. When I first read about this, I had one of those "aha" moments: if we spend time in nature and allow our senses to reorient to natural surroundings, we can reconnect with and grow in our naturalist intelligence dimension.

You may be thinking, "Why on earth do I need eight levels of intelligence? I'd be happy with one that is in good working order!" There's one more piece to this puzzle you need to know. Gardner's research at Harvard, Project Zero, reported yet another fact about intelligence, this time a bit more alarming:

> Researchers found that up to age four, almost all the children were at the genius level, in terms of the multiple frames of intelligences.... By age twenty, the percentage of children at genius level was down to 10 percent, and over twenty, the genius level proportion of the subjects sank to 2 percent.*

There it is: we are not nuturing our own brain power—as if some of us didn't already know this! If there ever were a time in our lives when we needed this eighth level of intelligence, it's now.

Have I convinced you yet to step outdoors?

Perhaps you're thinking that the idea of finding yourself in nature sounds nice in theory, but that actually *doing* it is another matter. It's easy to slip into the ready means of relaxation offered by our culture, ranging from a night of TV to an afternoon of shopping, from a weekend escape (to a hotel, where you'll probably still be indoors!) to a weeklong vacation (with its bookend pressures to make the preparations ahead of time and catch up with everything when you return). But rather than feeling refreshed and refueled after these escapes, it's all too probable that you will return to your ordinary routine still feeling drained

We are continually articulating the intelligence of the planet, which has grown up through all the species. The whole earth lives in us, and in every moment, we are both its creators and discoverers. We need only to reawaken these early memories.

—VALERIE ANDREWS,
SISTERS OF THE EARTH

---

* As reported in Peter Senge et al., *Presence: Human Purpose and the Field of the Future* (Cambridge, MA: The Society for Organizational Learning, Inc. 2004).

on some level. You muddle on, but your parched soul still longs for reunion with your passionate self.

You're not alone. In his fascinating book *Last Child in the Woods,* Richard Louv describes a phenomenon of our culture that he calls a "nature-deficit disorder." As our technologically advanced children spend more and more time in front of a screen, and less and less time climbing a tree or fishing in a river, they pay a price for this alienation from nature. Louv's list is scary: "diminished use of the senses, attention difficulties, and higher rates of physical and emotional illnesses ... tunneled senses, and feelings of isolation and containment." Might this be happening to you, as an adult, as well?

Looking at the flip side, however, Louv goes on to say, "Nature inspires creativity in a child by demanding visualization and the full use of the senses." This statement is for you, too! You can reconnect with the lovely, radiant, creative self you once were through nature. I believe that with all of my heart and mind, and I invite you to the adventure of restoring your wellspring to its original flowing state.

The Wellspring of Life

In SPA Sisters, we take our cue from the ancient wisdom of Proverbs: "Above all else, guard your heart, for it is the wellspring of life" (4:23 NIV).

To reverse our troubles, we must learn to reconnect with nature.

—MICHAEL COHEN,
RECONNECTING
WITH NATURE

I have seen this rebirth of sensory aliveness and keen alertness happen time and again in myself and others. Once this occurs, we can consciously choose, as well as expand, our modes of perception.

—STEVEN HARPER,
ECOPSYCHOLOGY

Think of your wellspring as a metaphor for the condition of your spirit. How clear or cloudy is it? How many layers of muck has life on this broken planet built up? How blocked are your streams of energy and creativity? No matter what the state of your wellspring is, the condition is not hopeless. Listen carefully: *If you can remember the clear, fresh wellspring you started with, you can restore it.* The path to clearing your wellspring is almost literally a "path"—any path that will take you outdoors.

In nature you have access to a part of yourself that you may have forgotten or that may have gotten lost in the stream of life. And in nature you have more access to your *memories* of being in nature. That's a valuable gift because as you are able to re-access your childlike sensate experiences, you will be able to connect with those core qualities that make up the real you.

In the book of Job is an ancient truth that I believe we each knew as children, before we got caught up in the rush to live: "Ask the animals, and they will teach you. Ask the birds of the sky, and they will tell you" (12:7 NLT). Children are incredibly present to the moment and to their senses. They see, hear, touch, taste, and smell their environment with immediacy. By being fully immersed in nature, in your senses, you can get back to this wonder of your lively, whole self.

In SPA Sisters, we help women restore their blocked wellsprings by starting with the question, "Who was I before my wellspring became blocked?" We ask each woman to recall an early memory of being outdoors, a memory that tells them something about their original senses and natural connection with the earth, something that tells them who they were before their wellspring became unclear. And, as you might guess, we ask them to go outside, to allow nature to awaken these memories.

Over and over again, I have heard women return to describe how being conscious and aware of nature helped them re-access their childhood memories in a sensate, present-oriented way. They describe vivid scenes of exploration, surprise, delight, contentment—a natural way of being at one with the earth. And, most important, they recognize at some deep level that what was true about their child self is still true for them today. For many, this is the start of a rich spiritual journey of reclaiming their authentic self.

Nature Memories

As women, giving voice to our stories is one of the ways we help each other learn and grow, and I feel especially privileged to have shared stories with many wonder-filled SPA Sisters. When friends hear our stories, they chuckle and say we sound like a bunch of children! I believe this is partially because each of us tells our story in a childlike, sensate way, describing sights, sounds, colors, and textures carefully. That these memories are so lively even now suggests how much meaning is encompassed in each experience, after many decades. As you read these recollections, listen for the sensate qualities, the child voice, the childlike energy coming through. We were not making an attempt to polish our stories, but to tell them in the present moment.

I'll start with Eileen, who was one of the original SPA Sisters. Her story about riding a bike wonderfully conveys a sense of her inner desire for freedom:

Worlds can be found by a child and an adult bending down and looking together under the grass stems or at the skittering crabs in a tidal pool.

——MARY CATHERINE
BATESON

The first memory I have is moving to the new house in Des Plaines from an apartment in Chicago. In Des Plaines we could be outside, we could play in the streets, on the grass, on the sidewalk and run around. There was much more spaciousness and fresh air. I remember things like playing hopscotch and jump rope, and just being outside riding bikes. I have a vivid memory of one of the first times I rode my bike alone. I remember riding along on a path. I had a feeling of freedom. I could go on my bike and just be outside roaming around. I felt safe and I felt free, and I remember thinking I would remember that moment for a long time. I had a feeling of being alive.

Eileen's sister Patty Martindale, who is also an original SPA Sister, has a gift of intuition and care for those she works with in her retail career. I love Patty's story because it conveys a special moment in time when a small girl ponders the biggest questions we have about life:

My brother was always very interested in space, and the big space program was going on in the sixties. I remember sometimes going out in the backyard. We'd be lying on the grass and it would be nighttime. We'd be looking up at the stars, and my brother would tell me how far away the stars were and that some of the stars were bigger than our sun. That really affected me, thinking about how big the universe was. Who created all this? How did this all come about? It made me feel so close to God. Feeling there was a big power was hard to absorb at such a young age. But I felt very close to nature and very close to the earth, even though I felt very small. I also felt part of it all. There was a lot more to our world than I was aware of. Hearing how intricate it was ... how creative this God was that created it ... how exciting it all was ... I loved knowing more about it.

Another original SPA Sister, Susan Schor, who was formerly a college professor and now works in the corporate world, remembered her childhood summers camping in the Catskill Mountains. Maybe you'll catch the sense of peace, comfort, and the sacred in her recollection:

My first recognition of the importance of nature was when I was a child in summer camp. I started camp when I was five. I loved camping out. I loved it when we got to sleep in the tents. We had these big tents with wooden floors that fit six or eight people, and there was always the option to sleep out under the stars. I liked to sleep out under the stars. It was

When I was four years old ... I was brought from Boston to this my native town, through these very woods and this field to the pond. It is one of the oldest scenes stamped on my memory.... Tonight my flute has waked the echoes over that very water.

—HENRY DAVID THOREAU

63

just something that felt miraculous, being out there. It wasn't just the sleeping or just the stars; there's some strong feeling that I have about the trees. Arriving and setting up my little life among the trees, setting up my sleeping bag, creating my little place, being around my friends, not having any walls, having a big natural opening, loving the trees and being amidst them. I remember sitting on my sleeping bag, reading, and talking with my friends. What I remember most is lying there and looking at the stars, and waking up to the stillness in the air and the dew. I remember lying there and looking up and seeing the treetops and part of the sky.

Another original SPA Sister, Sandy Alcorn, who has now retired from her work as dean of a master's program in social work, recalled her childhood experience with a waterfall. Her awareness of her senses is as fresh and alive today as it was then:

I have a summer memory of going swimming every afternoon, and one of my favorite experiences was sitting on a rock. They were the kind of slanted, big slabs of rocks that you could lay out on. I'd be lying there and the water would be rippling down the stone like a spring. If I put my head down, the water would just jump over me. I'd be a part of the waterfall. I could sit there forever and breathe because the water would bounce off the rock behind me and go right over me. I would just sit there in the sun having a great time. It was like being one with the water.

You've already heard from Anne at the opening of this chapter, but there's one more glimmer I'd like you to catch. Even when childhood memories are not all positive, there is still much to learn from these precious memories:

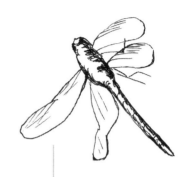

I was an energetic girl who wasn't fearful of the leeches and water moccasins in the jade-colored waters of the swampy parts of the backyard forest in my Maryland. The forest was filled with adventures. Vines hanging from places too high up there to see were waiting to be tested for swing strength by my hot and sweaty hands. Out there I was learning and made the rules.

But some lessons were painful: Don't remove a bunny from the nest because you can't feed it, and it will die. Don't touch baby birds because the parent birds will not come back. Don't remove egg sacks or break open tadpole sacks or they will die. I learned that the natural balance is delicate. I learned I had the power to kill in my ignorance. I chose to respect life. I examined and learned to "do no harm!" Early on, the urge to "own" the life I found was replaced by a need to understand and to return my captures to their original locations ... although there were exceptions to that rule, too!

It was fun to play with the rolly-polly potato bugs and use them as marbles when they curled into armor-plated balls. Catching a dragonfly was hard to do but not an experience to be scorned. A spool of Mom's good thread in one hand, with the other end tied around a dragonfly, turned into hours of fun-simulated flight

At times I feel as if I am spread out over the landscape and inside things, and am myself living in every tree, in the splashing of the waves, in the clouds and the animals that come and go, in the procession of the seasons.

—CARL JUNG

control long before gas- and electric-powered toy airplanes with wire con-
trols. Bees could also be fun if you removed the stinger with a stick and then
threw them on an older sister and her friends. Yes, there were some impor-
tant exceptions to the rules with excellent perks ...

When I was nine, we moved from this adventure land. Actually, it was
great timing; a developer had purchased the creek and woods. A commu-
nity pool was going to be built there, so they were dredging up my beloved
wilderness. I remember the day the bulldozer burrowed through the creek
and streams, churning the water into sticky brown mud. The wake of
destruction teemed with tadpoles sucking for air with "O" shaped mouths
as their bodies were entombed in molded clay caskets that hardened under
the hot sun. Everyone said it would be better for the neighborhood, but my
soul cried at the casualties that day. What was going to happen to my
beloved amphibians, reptiles, and insects? I remember our car pulling out
of the driveway, never to return. I sat in the front seat with tears, holding
my banana road snack.

Now, I believe I was blessed to have experienced the best of that place
before rural became urban. I have never returned.

And, then, there is my own story. One day I went outdoors to do the Wellspring
exercise of recalling a childhood memory and was drawn to some rocks in a shallow
part of the river. As the water washed around them, I noticed that there were patches
of color showing through the muck, and I remembered this scene from my childhood:

My father's farm was outside of town, near Edgar, Wisconsin, and we
were driving there in his wonderful hog-smelling truck. I was around four

years old and felt excited, knowing we were near as we passed Pete's Bar. When we reached the farm, I raced down to the icy cold creek, full of anticipation and excitement. I can still see the clear water dancing over the rocks. I was delighted as I noticed small pop bottles chilling. I thought they grew there! I later found out that my father had put them in the stream to chill.

When I think of that recollection, I still smile. If you let your mind drift back over the years, I know there are some memories for you to reclaim that will enrich your life today with the energy of your child self.

The world will never starve for wonder, but only for want of wonder.

—G. K. CHESTERSON

And the end of all our exploring
Will be to arrive where we started
And know the place for the first time.

—T. S. ELIOT,
"THE WASTE LAND"

An Energizing Experience

For this experience, gather what you need to be comfortable outdoors. If it's winter, bundle up with a favorite hat, scarf, and mittens; if it's summer, your outdoor venture may call for less clothing and more sunscreen. Whatever the weather is, give some thought to what would make you as comfortable as possible in the elements. Then collect your journal, crayons, pencil, and whatever else you would like to take along.

Ready? Find a place outdoors where you can be quiet and attentive to the nature around you, as well as to your thoughts. Settle yourself someplace where you can relax and become aware of your breathing. Then ease into this meditative exercise: I put myself into a contemplative mood. I look slowly, carefully, taking in what I see, one thing at a time. I listen with sensitive ears to what I hear, becoming more conscious of the many layers of sound as time passes. I take in deep breaths of air, focusing on each distinct smell I am able to sense. I become aware of how my body feels, of what is touching me.

As you pay thoughtful attention, look and listen for something in nature that attracts you. Where does your attention rest? What seems to call to you?

When you find yourself drawn to something, think about how you are connected to it. What does it say about where you

I believe that there is a subtle magnetism in Nature, which, if we unconsciously yield to it, will direct us aright.

—Henry David Thoreau

68

are in your life right now? Take some time to enjoy and experience the moment.

Then allow yourself to become centered and think of an early recollection in nature, some experience that you had as a child that involved being outdoors, interacting with the natural world. When a memory surfaces, consider these two questions:

- What does this recollection tell me about who I was before my wellspring became unclear?

- What is the contrast between my childhood memory and where I am right now in my life?

You are a child of the universe, no less than the trees and the stars.

—DESIDERATA

As you can tell from the SPA Sisters stories in this chapter, many women find it helpful to write a description of their memories in their journals, with as much detail as they can remember. This is an excellent way to capture the alive sense of how you experienced the world as a child. Don't try to polish your writing; keep your words as close to your natural childlike state as possible.

Then take some time to reflect on how you feel about this memory. Use meditation (just being in the moment, aware of your senses), art, journal writing, poetry, movement—however you feel moved to respond.

When you are ready to return to your everyday life, take a moment to give thanks for the inner beauty you were born with.

If you are undertaking this retreat with others, gather in a circle when you come back together and give each woman plenty of time to reflect and to share whatever she desires about her experience, without advising, judging, or attempting to fix her. If someone desires a response, share only out of your own experience, perhaps with a recollection of your own that helps you relate to her. Remember, it is sometimes a good thing to have one person loosely leading so that all have time to be heard. When everyone has finished, you might want to take time to name the things you are grateful for that have come out of this time together.

If you are undertaking these experiences one week at a time, use the following activity for the time in between: Spend an intentional period of time in nature this week. Pay attention to what you are drawn to in your surroundings and what it says about what you are currently experiencing in your life. Be aware of any childlike energy you feel. Journal or create something about your experience. If you are participating in this exploration with others, bring something from your experience to share at the start of your next meeting.

FOUR
Transforming
OPENING TO POSSIBILITIES

Making Way

Do you love a warming fire? Coming in from in the cold to a cozy room with logs crackling in the fireplace, flames leaping up to greet you—this is the stuff of holiday cards and winter daydreams. Roaring fires that burn beyond our control, however, are something else altogether. They're downright scary. Yet that is exactly what happened on the midwestern prairie— and what helped create some of the richest soil in the world. Most likely started by lightning strikes, or by Native American peoples who wanted to herd buffalo and make way for new lush prairie to entice small game, the raging fires that burned across the prairies were unbelievably intense. Old journals describe walls of fire over forty feet high that created a deafening sound.

Yet the prairie burns, as they were called, were vital to the development of the prairie ecosystem. After a burn, the prairie would appear to be a black, stubby mess ... but only for a time. The charred prairie was actually an empty palette readying itself for next year's abundance. The blackened state was the beginning of transformation. Far below the surface, the grasses with deep root systems not only survived but were reinvigorated to send up more and stronger growth. Some of the plants had such tough seed pods that they *needed* the heat of the fire to break open so new life could emerge. Still other plants—the unwanted invaders—were burned off, making room for indigenous plants that were at risk of getting crowded out.

It's not surprising that the Potawatomi word for prairie translates as "burnt-over bare ground." But what rich barrenness. Though the post-burn land would not look like much, the exposed soil was ready for the warmth of the sun to call forth a bounty of blooms. Through the transformation of the burn, the prairie gained strength. Even today, people involved in prairie restoration projects will tell you that a prescribed burn is one of the crucial elements in keeping the prairie healthy.

When Leon and I were working on our prairie restoration project at Prairie Lake, we would schedule a burn each spring. A prairie burn is not a matter of simply going out and lighting a match; it is a planned effort for a particular result. Leon would mow a ten-foot-wide strip around the edge of the prairie to create

Had there been no fires, these fine prairies, so marked a feature of the country, would have been covered by the heaviest forest.

—ALDO LEOPOLD,
A SAND COUNTY ALMANAC

a firebreak. He'd also check the weather parameters for low wind conditions, gather torches and rakes, and get permission from the local fire department. The preparation made the burn safe and was a necessary part of the transformation that was to come, for the lesson of the prairie is clear: change is needed for growth to happen.

As human beings, we are constantly growing and transforming. Transformation is essential for our growth and health, just as it is for the prairie, though we have an uneasy relationship with it because of the unpredictability of the fires of change. Eileen captures some of this paradox in her description of her feelings about change:

> *I love beauty, but I love nature even when it's not beautiful. I like the flowers when they're dying; I find them beautiful. I like the change. I realize that I thrive on it and yet I'm terrified. It's like that sometimes with my clothing line. We're always in that transition. It always feels like it's moving toward this and then it's moving toward that.... There are always things that I want to change.*

Personally, I am somewhat resistant to change. I have a tendency to get cozy. I even joke occasionally that I am glad "cozy" hasn't been identified as an addiction because I would be in trouble. If you were to come to my home, you would probably look around,

My inner changes and emotions were often triggered by the land: I would feel the breakthrough of the spring as the windswept sky and a sudden movement of the clouds brought forth a new round of activity.

—VALERIE ANDREWS,
SISTERS OF THE EARTH

73

take a deep, satisfying breath, and think, "comfy, cozy." When I look back at my life, I understand why cozy feels so important to me. After a childhood marked by chaos, divorce, a lengthy hospitalization, living with relatives, and being out of touch with my dear father for eighteen years, my primary goal as an adult was to create a safe nest and a "happy family."

Fortunately, as an adult I've also come to know that there is something rooted far deeper in me than my need for cozy. With my faith perspective, I have come to believe that God has something much greater in mind for me, for each of us—freedom. I read in the book of Galatians that "it is for freedom that Christ has set us free.... do not let yourselves be burdened again by a yoke of slavery" (5:1 NIV). I trust that God has a larger vision for my life, and I need to be willing to change so I do not go back into the slavery of a too-small life. I have learned to (somewhat) willingly be present, no matter what is going on. I know that everything is usable and goodness will come out of each moment, whether it seems good or bad at the time. And, gradually, I have learned through the process of my life that it is all good.

One of the important stories of the Hebrew Bible describes a dramatic moment when God parted the Red Sea, making a pathway for the Israelites to escape from their slavery under Pharaoh. Whenever I hear that story, I am reminded of how much courage it took for these scared people to trust the path of change God was providing for them. Even though they desperately wanted to escape their old life, and probably knew that

And this, our life, exempt from public haunt, finds tongues in trees, books in the running brooks, sermons in stones, and good in everything.

—WILLIAM SHAKESPEARE

almost anything would be better than being Pharaoh's slaves, still, they had to be willing to let go of the known, predictable past and step into an absolutely unknown future: How could they escape? Where would they go? How would they live?

My husband and I have been honored to be part of several Passover Seders, the Jewish ritual that commemorates this liberation. One of the Seder songs, "Dayenu," lists each thing that God did to make freedom from the Egyptians possible. After each proclamation, the refrain is essentially, "That would have been enough." Yet the song continues because God kept doing more. That is not only my experience in life but also what helps me when I get scared about change. Each time I tentatively approach the next step of transformation in my life, I remember that God has already brought me through the Red Sea, so to speak. I trust God to keep doing more, even though what is up ahead is unknown, even though I might dig in my heels a bit at first.

Even with these reminders, change can still be difficult. Clearing out the old to make way for the new requires preparation and effort. Each time you prepare to move into what's next, it is important to remember that you are protecting and restoring your heart, your core, your wellspring. When you believe you have value to your core, then you can open to bigger possibilities; change becomes less of a problem and more of a promise of what's to come.

That promise is something of what Deb experienced while clearing out debris and weeds to create space for a healing garden.

I have learned … to value change that is not sudden or ill-considered but grows out of the ground of experience.

—KATHLEEN NORRIS

75

To sit in the shade on a fine day and look upon verdure is the most perfect refreshment.

—JANE AUSTEN

Cleaning out the brush wasn't easy, but it not only created space for daffodils to come up in the spring, it also opened up an area for meditation where Deb could enjoy the spaciousness as a symbol of her openness to renewal:

In the clearing the sun warms my back
in the golden hour before the sun sets.
As the cool fall wind blows through this cleared
space, the leaves rustle and crackle.

Covered for years
with vines, dead branches, and scrub brush,
the trees whisper their thanks.

The leaves are falling, stripping the trees.
How wonderful that I can now see their form and
shape.
I can see through the woods and beyond
to the railroad tracks.

I want to be like the trees, stripped bare, naked—
free, unencumbered.
A clean space ready
for renewal, rest and relaxation—
making way for a deeper Spirit Place
to fill the empty space.

Alive with Possibilities

I am always learning something new about transformation in the mirror of nature. In the Midwest we have dramatic seasonal changes, and I have the opportunity to watch transformation year round. If there's one thing I've learned, it's that change is unpredictable. The dictionary tells me that, in the northern hemisphere, spring stretches from March through April and May. Astronomically, I'm told, spring starts with the vernal equinox on March 21. Yet the transformation into spring is a capricious process, regardless of what the dictionary or the calendar have to say about it. After a long, cold winter, it might be icy on March 21, but I don't get into a tizzy because I know it is all part of the transformation process and that spring *will* arrive. I have seen the sweet apple green of new spring come and go over many years, and I know it will come again.

When I re-recognize the positive nature of transformation, I am able to be more open to it. I can reflect on the spiritual path of change: to trust that change is part of the cycle of God's faithfulness, to believe that something new is coming, and to have faith that each moment, big or small, is alive with possibilities.

Some transformations are dramatic, like the walls of fire that ancient prairie burns created. Some transformations require a lot of prep work, clearing out old debris, weeding, amending the soil, aerating the packed earth. Other transformations are much more subtle, requiring nothing more—and nothing less—than a willingness on our part to put ourselves on the path, to make ourselves available to change.

This frame of reference has turned my life into a remarkable adventure full of learning and meaning. Just today, as I was thinking about transformation, a simple thing happened in my household that reminded me anew that even small, everyday occurrences offer the potential for transformation.

Don't be in a rush to tell Nature what you already know or feel. The more you "speak" at the outset, the more Nature will remain silent.... Devote your energy to maintaining your state of alertness, vulnerability, and response-ability.

—PETER LONDON,
DRAWING CLOSER TO NATURE

Leon invited me to go outside with him to watch for deer coming in to feed on corn at our neighbor Bob's house—in twenty-degree weather with fresh snow. You see, Leon had just been inspired to erect his newly purchased two-person tree stand high up in a tree in the middle of the fifty-acre woods behind us. Given my increasing interest in nature, he thought I'd love to sit out there with him. The problem was, I felt perfectly cozy in my indoor nest, and I wanted to continue writing.

After a slight interior flinch, I said I'd go. I put on my super outdoor gear, complete with a cat-burglar face mask and my microwaveable mittens. We ventured out and I made my way up the ladder high into the tree. Once we were perched on the stand, I turned to look at Leon; rarely have I seen my husband so delighted. Sitting there in his camouflage jacket, with rosy cheeks and a grin from ear to ear, he seemed very pleased to have lured me into his world. Next to this man, I am truly a beginner in the world of solitude. He can sit in a boat all day, catch no fish, and totally enjoy himself. I think *he* thinks I might finally be ready!

It was 3:45 p.m., and there we sat, waiting.

As I looked at the black tree trunks popping out from the white snow, I found myself thinking about this particular season of the year, the time of Advent in the Christian church—a time of waiting, of preparation for the coming Christ child. I found myself praying for new birth in my own life.

And we waited. Pretty soon it was 4:45 p.m. Nature man sat there still smiling, still glad to have me there.

Just then, two deer came out. One pranced along a path twenty feet from us, stopping directly in front of our tree stand. He looked up for a long moment, then ran in the opposite direction, snorting and huffing, white tail up. He must have been announcing our presence to the rest of the herd because they did not venture in for dinner until we had returned home.

It was a simple experience, yes, but a transformation nonetheless. You see, transformation does not always have to be about the big stuff. It can happen one small shift at a time. As I sat in that tree and prayed about new birth in my life, I became aware that the very act of sitting in a tree stand with Leon was new. I had been consciously wanting to be more a part of his world, and in this quiet hour spent in the tree stand, I had moved a little closer. When we got back to the house, he said, "Welcome to my planet," and he is now referring to me as his "tree climber."

Sometimes making space for transformation requires not so much *preparation* as *readiness,* not so much *effort* as *openness.* Sometimes we simply need to place ourselves in the path so we will be ready for change when it comes our way.

My friend Pam Allnutt, who works as art teacher/professor and deeply expresses herself as a painter and poet, came to SPA Sisters at a time when she was thinking of making a transition in her life. Her journal entry about deep listening holds a glimpse of what it means to be open to whatever change is coming:

Yet, when I allowed my eyes to look truly in the way nature had taught me, with beginner eyes, I could see that it was thriving beyond all my expectations.

—SUSAN SCOTT,
HEALING WITH NATURE

Umbrella in hand, I slide open the glass door to the patio and step out into the sleet-like snow. My boots make splashing noises across the pavement of the parking lot. It's not a quiet snow. It plops as it hits the ground.

Gingerly crossing Butterfield Road, I enter Herrick Lake Forest Preserve, a favored place of refuge. Today, however, traffic sounds mar the air with an insistent hum. I'm annoyed. I start walking briskly.

There are only two other sets of footprints on the newly covered path. A single hiker circling twice? I stand in a print ... my foot engulfed. Ice covering the lake speaks subtly, revealing its depth in variations of gray. Ripples texture the surface as though stilled at play by an arctic beast ... claws marking a trail across the span of frozen water.

Halfway around the lake, a thicket of purple stems twist, snaring my baggage of deadlines and errands. Lighter now, I linger, my steps slowing. Nearby, cattails bend low listening to the fluid music of icebound waters.

Approaching the bridge, my feet slip on a gentle rise. A small path forks into the woods. Pausing, I close my umbrella to enter the narrow space. Branches tug at my coat as I push my way deeper into the forest. Soon, the trail opens into a small clearing. My breath stills.

There is only the dripping of trees. Fallen logs lay scattered under fresh white blankets. I look up through fingers of branches, heavy snow stinging my cheeks. The wind rises as russet leaves weave round me.

I hear.

Many of us have forgotten the value of quiet listening as preparation for change. Recently, I was running a retreat by a river, and I asked the participants to close their eyes as I led them in a meditation. I, too, closed my eyes—

and was surprised to suddenly become aware of the sound of the river rushing, the ducks quacking, and the competitive traffic noise in the distance. I had noticed none of these until my eyes were closed, and I became more present.

Being quiet in nature, in a meditative, conscious way, invites listening. For me, it is a form of prayer. As an extrovert, I have the urge to talk. When a friend gave me an article on listening prayer, I realized that if I was *talking* to God, I wasn't *listening*. I know that sounds elementary, but I needed a little shake-up in that area, so I began on a path of listening prayer. I often use my journal for this prayer form because it corrals my extrovert nature. First, I write down what's on my mind (sometimes with a grateful heart, sometimes in a whiny voice) and then I pray for God's protection (so I and anyone else will get out of the way). Then, when my mind is finally quiet, I ask what God has to say.

Listening is literally at the heart of many ancient spiritual practices, such as *lectio divina,* a method of meditating on the scriptures and waiting for God to speak. Or the prophet Isaiah's succinct admonition in the Hebrew Bible: "Listen, so that you may live" (Isaiah 55:3 NRSV). From the early monastics to Saint Francis, quieting the heart and listening for God has been the purpose of solitude. In his later years, twentieth-century Trappist monk and scholar Thomas Merton, who wrote more than sixty books during his lifetime, became much less interpretive and more attentive. In *Thoughts in Solitude,* he said simply, "My life is a listening.... My salvation is to hear and respond."

As you devote your mind and body and spirit to the deepening of your acquaintance with Nature, the more finely made structures of Nature become discernible. The more you look, the more you see. The more you listen, the more you hear.

—PETER LONDON,
DRAWING CLOSER
TO NATURE

81

In our contemporary culture, Dr. Llewellyn Vaughn-Lee, a Jungian psychologist who uses an ancient Sufi approach to silent meditation, also teaches that listening is a way of praying: "Listening is not an effort, not a technique; it is not work to be done. Listening springs from the desire to be with the one whom you wait to hear."

Theologian Harvey Cox wrote, "If you are trying to learn something from people, you have to listen to them and stifle the impulse to think about what you are going to say next." Maybe it's something like this with transformation: If we are trying to change something in our lives, we need to stop and *listen,* to stifle the impulse about what we are going to *do* next. Sometimes transformation is more about being present than planning what to do.

When conservationist Wendell Berry left the city for his rural roots, he found in the country a richness that was "inexhaustible ... in all its possibilities. I walked over it, looking, listening, smelling, touching, alive to it as never before." Berry's approach may well be our way to transformation: be open to all its possibilities, be alive to it as never before.

Surprise! Surprise!

I love to set the table for guests, savoring the way everything looks and tastes. (I don't really want to admit how many sets of dishes and terrific table cloths I have.) If you were to take away all else from me in the course of cooking, please leave me with

We first thought of presence as being fully conscious and aware in the present moment. Then we began to appreciate presence as deep listening, of being open beyond one's preconceptions and historical ways of making sense.

—PRESENCE

garlic, olive oil, and balsamic vinegar. I can take these three simple ingredients and sauté a variety of brightly colored veggies, along with, let's say, a few fresh Gulf shrimp, and produce an amazing dish. And then there's roasted garlic. The taste is nothing short of miraculous. The heat of roasting can transform this hard little bulb into something mellow and sweet and flavorful. Some have even called roasted garlic a "miracle food."

That's a little of the nature of transformation. Sometimes, when and where we least expect it—with ordinary people in everyday places—something amazing happens. Delightfully, surprisingly, the alchemy of transformation pulls together the common stuff of life to create something fresh in our lives.

I think of my friend Sandy, who, during her tenure as the dean of a master's program in social work, participated in a program that provided grants to five different organizations. She was part of the group that visited each site to see how the program was being implemented in each place. Usually when they arrived at a site, they would sit in meetings and listen to prepared reports. Or the people they were visiting would take them on a tour, describing what they were doing with the kids in the program and what activities the grant was being used for. However, when they visited a Native American group in Santa Fe, instead of being presented with reports, they were handed small sketch pads and pencils, taken in a car out to a river, and told by their escort to "sketch and find your place and come back and talk about it." Cheerily, he added, "I'll see you in two hours," and left.

You can imagine the group's surprise; this was not at all what they had expected! Was this supposed to be "the program"?

Later, when Sandy told the man that this was the most unusual experience she had ever had on a grant site visit, he simply said, "This is the way we reach our people. Yes, we have schools, but we have to get into their way of knowing their world."

Sit down before facts like a child, and be prepared to give up every preconceived notion, follow humbly wherever and to whatever abysses Nature leads, or you shall learn nothing.

—THOMAS HUXLEY

For Sandy and the team, the shift from the usual academic framework into the Native American way of knowing in nature was a transformative experience. Instead of seeing a replica of the mainstream cultural message—that we need more information— they encountered the spiritual lesson that we each have what we need inside, if we take the time and make the space to find it.

This kind of internal knowing requires awareness and opening to our senses. When we allow nature to be our teacher, we create an internal space where we can sit with our own chaos and unformed ideas. We make a choice to be still, to be expectant of what is to come.

For me, this choice includes trusting that The Artist has much more in mind for me than I can imagine. I have wonderful people, things, and circumstances in my life, and yet, without God, I know my interior life would close down like a circus folding and going to the next town. When I remember this lesson—and, eventually, I always do—I can be open to whatever is ahead. By choosing to participate in the co-creation of my life, I become a willing participant in change.

During one Wellspring Group, after considering this idea of being open to transformation, I opened to the landscape around me and began writing in my journal:

It is spring, but everything is still brown ... holding on. I see two geese paddling to stay upstream on the river and then letting go and riding the waves down-

stream. It reminds me of the outrigger canoes on Waikiki Beach. It strikes me that there is a promise in the bleak, barren, brown stalks of early spring. I just picked a purple cone-flower stem loaded with seeds for the future.
Spring brown stalks
Crowned
Bursting with seeds
Containing
Future visions and dreams.
    The brown stalks with seed head tops remind me that life, then death, is the path to resurrection.

I like the way the opening of the book *Presence* describes the potential of a seed: "The seed is a gateway through which the future possibility of the living tree emerges." I'm reminded of the seeds that were hand-gathered from ancient prairie remnants to start our prairie restoration project at Prairie Lake. Over the years the prairie had many surprises for us, but by the ninth growing season I had given up on ever see-ing the lush iridescent orange of the butterfly weed plant emerge from the seeds we had sown. I went out and purchased twelve butterfly weed forbs and planted them strategically so I could see them from the house.

But the prairie held one more surprise. That ninth summer, way out in the mid-dle of the prairie, far from the house, four jewel-like butterfly weed plants, complete with butterflies, bloomed for the first time from the seeds planted so many growing seasons back.

Nature's message is powerful: trust the seeds of transformation within you; many beautiful surprises await.

The Beautiful In-between

Nature is an amazing model of transformation. The process seems so gracious, with no fussing. I think of the exquisite designs on the white sand beaches of Dauphin Island. The lights and shadows cast amazing patterns on the parallel zigs and zags of sand, and I could be quite content painting them for the rest of my life. And then the winds and tides change and an entirely new and equally beautiful pattern emerges. Sandpipers and other birds scurry along the beach, weaving in and out, disappearing before a storm, and getting right back to it afterward. The transformation seems as automatic and natural as breathing. There is a rhythm to it that all of nature seems to remember—except us. And we *can* remember.

Nature is always in the moment and does not seem to judge a particular moment as more important than another. We, on the other hand, seem to excel at holding nearly unattainable goals in front of us and missing the moments on the way there. I love the way Eileen seems to live in her many moments. When I call her, it is not uncommon for her to ask me to call back in a bit because she and the kids are "having a moment." For Eileen, what happens in the moment is important:

> When people ask me if the house is finished, I'll say, yes, I guess it's finished, but there are always things I want to change. What I'm trying to do is accept and

I had to learn how to look closely at what was so, question my preconceived assumptions, then welcome the new life that followed as it did in nature.

—Susan Scott,
Healing with Nature

enjoy the in-between moments. Nature shows me that all the time ... it's not the perfect hydrangeas, the perfect roses, the perfect green grass, and the perfect blooming tree all happening at the same time. It's more like, this one is blooming, and these are dying, and you have to get the heads off those, and other things are coming up. I don't know much about gardens, but I know there's a peak moment for which people design gardens. What about the other 364 days of the year? Nature is imperfect, it's always changing. It's peaking and growing, and that's the truth of it.

I experience this constant change and growth in my work and with my kids because it's life. It's never finished and never perfect. If you plant a gorgeous garden and you have a vision that it's going to be "perfect" at the peak moment, and the peak moment comes and it isn't, maybe that's okay. Maybe it was more beautiful in the in-between moments.

When I am alone the flowers are really seen; I can pay attention to them.... They live and die in a few days; they keep me closely in touch with process, with growth, and also with dying.

—MAY SARTON

"Beautiful in the in-between moments." Isn't that a great description of the process of transformation? Yet when we're in the middle of change—shifting from one place to another, reaching one goal and moving on to the next, getting through one adjustment only to face yet another—it's not likely that we're going to be thinking, "This is *beautiful*."

It's time to reconsider.

If there is any doubt in your mind about the beauty of transformation, think about autumn. Many consider this season of change from the explosion of summer growth to the winter dormancy ahead the most beautiful of all the seasons. When we lived at Prairie Lake, my heart used to ache with the beautiful sound of the cottonwood leaves blowing and crinkling like paper as they turned bright yellow in the fall.

Patty captures some of the glory of fall yellows in her memory of hiking in the woods on Lake Superior:

> *I was really attracted to the intense colors of the trees. We got far back on the hiking trail, and the sun was still out. We were in a heavy forested area where the trees were all similar types, all bright yellow. The ground was covered by yellow leaves, and it was like yellow carpeting. The sun was coming through the trees and that was yellow, too. I was in this whole yellow place, and I felt God's presence so much there. Everything about this yellow and bright and cheerful place made me think of God. This was an intense realization of God being so bright. It was a profound moment for me.*

Patty's words remind me of a line Matthew Fox wrote about the medieval mystic Hildegard of Bingen: "Hildegard's picturing of the universe bathed in gold is her way of celebrating creation's glory, the presence of God throughout creation."

Deb had a similar joyous experience when she attended a Wellspring Group one fall. She began to do crayon tracings of leaves and found herself "marveling at the variety in shape, color, size, and texture. I feel as if I have returned to my childhood, picking up these treasures to show my mother and teachers." Her lines of poetry capture not only the beauty but the power of transformation:

LEAVES OF FALL

Falling from heaven
gracefully, effortlessly,
surrendering all
the leaves of fall.

Sunlit leaves of fall,
bright golden honey, blue sky
takes my breath away.

Jewels from heaven,
perfect symmetry, color,
beauty transformed.

Blessed leaves of fall
vibrant in your golden age,
letting go in the gentle breeze,
accepting, joyfully
this transformation,
giving life to the new generation.

Can you relate to this poem? Does something in you ache for change? Are you ready to embrace the beauty of change, to allow yourself to be present in all of your senses to the transformative moments of your life? Think of it this way: Your present is creating your future. Relish the moments; they are the signposts of your life. Your path to restoring your wellspring lies open before you.

This is the truth of the pervading intricacy of the world's detail: the creation is not a study, a roughed-in sketch; it is supremely, meticulously created, created abundantly, extravagantly, and in fine.

—ANNIE DILLARD

As we discover our rightful place in the world, break through the barriers of hand-me-down ideas and customs that have kept us from our ancient, infinite, dazzling family of origin in Nature, we newly experience ourselves and our world.

—PETER LONDON,
DRAWING CLOSER
TO NATURE

A Transforming Experience

Dress for the outdoors and take with you your journal and whatever pencils, pens, and art supplies you wish. Look for an area that you are drawn to and take time to enjoy being in the moment. Then let yourself ease into this meditative exercise: As I look around, I see many miracles, both large and small. I see constant change brought about by natural growth, by the wind, by the rotation of the earth, by the changing colors, by rainfall, all taking place with what seems to be an inherent orderliness. I see in nature the concepts of hope, strength, perseverance, and faith. I begin to wonder and am reminded of situations in my life that I want to change, but I haven't taken on that challenge yet.

Look around you once again. What is it about this area that draws you? Notice how you feel in your body as you allow yourself to be present in this moment, in this place. Then take a few minutes to reflect on these questions:

- Does the routine of my daily life leave me feeling empty?

- What are the unhealthy ways I try to fill myself (habits, passive activities, addictions)?

Think of something in your life you would like to see changed. Find a symbol of transformation you are attracted to in nature.

- How might this symbol represent a transformation I would like to make?

- How do I feel about transforming the condition of my wellspring?

Reflect on your response to these questions through art, journal writing, haiku, movement—whatever form you would like to use for expression. Then come to a place of stillness and ask yourself:

- What change—even a small one—can I begin to make so I am able to consider transforming my wellspring?

As you come to the close of your time in nature, be especially aware of how your body feels, where you notice any easing or any tension. Notice any particular emotions that are surfacing. Be graciously accepting of wherever you are on this path of change.

If you are undertaking this retreat with others, come back together in a circle and share your experience with the group, giving each woman time to relate whatever she wishes. If anyone wants a response, speak out of your own experience. Remember: this is a time for reflection, not advice or judgment or fixes. When everyone has finished, you might want to take time to name the things you are grateful for that have come out of this time together.

If you are undertaking these experiences one week at a time, use the following activity for the time in between: Take some time to connect to yourself in nature this week. Notice the transformations you see in nature and how they relate to your life. Think about one way you can begin to make a needed transformation in your life. If you are participating in this exploration with others, share some of your thoughts at the start of your next meeting.

We shrink from change; yet is there anything that can come into being without it? What does Nature hold dearer, or more proper to herself?

—Marcus Aurelius

91

FIVE
Clearing

LETTING GO OF THE OLD
TO MAKE WAY FOR THE NEW

God's Pruning Shears

Have you ever visited the eBay Internet auction website? If you've checked it out, you know how easy it is to shift from being a window shopper to a customer. Something inevitably shows up on the screen that you've "just got to have." I found that out when I saw my beloved dollhouse furniture from the fifties. I suddenly "needed" it for my newly redeemed dollhouse family, the Renwals, given to me by a friend who had learned how much I regretted losing them. I started with the living room and ended up buying a houseful of furniture—and even adding the baby of the family, who hadn't been part of my childhood collection.

What are your just-got-to-haves? Something for your antique collection? New clothes for the season? More books? Another plant for your garden? We tend to think of cravings in terms of

Prune and trim we must,

but not with ruthless

haste and ready prun-

ing knife,

until we have reflected

upon the tree we trim,

the environment it

lives in,

and the sap of life which

feeds it.

—THOMAS R. KELLY,
A TESTAMENT OF
DEVOTION

harmful stuff, such as drugs or alcohol or smoking. But even good things can complicate our lives when we come to believe we *need* it all—and more. (Actually, I am glad to have the Renwals back, but I *could* unload a few other items....) This makes me think of stories I've heard about people who face great odds to get to a treasure sunk in the ocean, and then drown because they are unable to haul it back up. Their unwillingness to let go costs them their lives.

John Michael Talbot—musician, monk, and mystic—has written, "Simplicity is God's grand antidote to a culture of money and madness. And properly understood and lived out, simplicity is God's pruning shear, which cuts back the tangled branches of our lives, enabling us to begin living freely, sharing generously, and living deeply." Ah, simplicity. The very word almost brings a sigh of relief. Simplifying has become very popular these days. Maybe we're finally getting it; maybe we're beginning to recognize that living in a sustainable way means giving up some things. But, as writer Daniel Quinn so poignantly states in his novel *Beyond Civilization,* "It doesn't occur to [us] that living in an unsustainable way is also about giving up things, very precious things like security, hope, light-heartedness, and freedom from anxiety, fear, and guilt."

When we begin to think of clearing out our wellspring, it's these "very precious things" that need our attention. When we recognize that our lives have gotten cluttered, we may welcome the idea of getting in there with a set of pruning shears to clear things out. But before we start madly pruning, we need to clarify what is important, what we want for our lives. A popular title humorously points to the obvious: *If You Don't Know Where You Are Going, You'll Probably End Up Somewhere Else.* To rephrase it in the positive, we need to know where we're going in order to get there.

If you are thinking about clearing out the old to make way for the new, you need to know what your priorities are. What would you like to make space *for*? What would promote a clear, flowing wellspring for you?

In our younger years, before life gets so crowded, it is easier to be in touch with our innate knowledge of what is important, as Eileen's words reveal:

> *I'm a water baby ... whether it's a trip to the Hamptons, to Florida or Mexico, walking on the beach is one of my favorite things to do. When I was a sophomore in high school, a bunch of us decided to walk to Lake Michigan. We walked along the road for twelve miles; we were heading to the water! I remember that I'd do anything to get to the lake.*

Even as a teenager in the Midwest, where getting to the water was not an easy task, Eileen listened to her instinctive, natural self and followed her urge to get to the lake, no matter what it took.

Depending on our age and circumstances, our priorities might not be so straightforward. There are tasks to complete, kids to feed,

This expanse of water was an inconceivable pleasure to me, an incomparable splendor. At that time the idea become fixed in my mind that I must live near a lake; without water, I thought, nobody could live at all.

—CARL JUNG

95

errands to run, bills to pay, meetings to attend, responsibilities to meet. Things pile up and the question of what's truly important gets buried in the accumulation of to-do lists and "stuff." Sometimes, we simply postpone the priority question, saying, "I'll think about it when I have time." Other times, such as during a crisis or at a decision-making crossroads, the "what's important" question suddenly becomes imperative.

Wherever you are in the prioritizing process, nature can be a wise guide for you, as Pam recognized when she attended a Wellspring Group:

> My experience in SPA Sisters came at a time when I was thinking of making a transition in my life. The process of spending time in nature, journaling, and then sharing what came to the surface with other women was a gift. Time spent meditating on what I observed cleared away debris that had piled up, and revealed to my opened eyes what was truly important. This made it much easier to take the necessary steps to change my situation.

As I listen to Pam's voice, I hear my own need to clear out, get beyond my busy day, and go to the quiet that nature offers.

> Slow down, hear the breeze
> I am calling to you now
> Always
> All days

Since you have picked up this book on nature-based spirituality, I assume that nature, in some way, also calls to you. Maybe you don't think of it as a call from God, but that's the way I hear it. When I am in a natural setting, I am making time to see, hear, and feel who I am—the person God created me to be—and to sense where I want to be moving in my life. If the key question is, "What are your priorities?" then I think the key answer lies in two additional questions: Where do you find yourself spiritually centered? When does your wellspring feel clear?

Letting Go of Busyness

Many years ago I was running a two-part retreat on letting go, and one woman lugged a huge, heavy purse into our first meeting. She explained that she was prepared for any eventuality and even had a first aid kit on hand. At the second meeting, she arrived with a tiny clutch. She looked radiant as she identified this change in handbags as a movement toward faith in her life. She said she was ready to travel light and count on God.

Letting go is always an ongoing choice, but we have to start somewhere. For many of us, one of the crucial places to begin is with our chronic busyness. Overflowing calendars, to-do lists, and appointments may well be among the greatest threats to a free-flowing wellspring.

I think busyness is a little like the invasive Canadian thistle that was accidentally introduced to the United States in the 1600s—and introduced to me when I was living on our prairie. A Canadian thistle plant produces around one million seeds in a season and is not only a vicious invader of a prairie landscape, but is also a tyrant to farmers, greatly reducing crop yields. The

Nature does not hurry, yet everything is accomplished.

—Lao Tzu

plant actually looks attractive at first, with its lovely lavender flower, but it is secretly getting ready to spread rhizomes and seeds that will eventually crowd out everything else. One website describes it as an "alien species that can change the natural structure of plant communities."

Canadian thistle is a serious management threat to even the most dedicated prairie restoration project. I have probably done at least a hundred hours of serious battle with this weed myself! Burnings help eliminate the invader, as well as repeated mowing, and I have personally pulled many hundreds out of the ground, but no one method is permanent. I once read an article by a fellow who recognized that he had a fierce crop of this thistle in a newly cut drainage ditch. The odd thing was that the thistle completely stopped growing past an invisible line in the dirt. He figured out that two soil types came together in this particular place, and that this thistle would not grow in the rich topsoil. Using a rich mulch, he eradicated it in several years.

Does this invasive plant sound at all like the items on your calendar or to-do list? Have one or two well-intentioned commitments spread into multiple projects that seem as if they're taking over your life? Are any "alien" agendas changing your "natural structure"? Maybe you've tried to weed out a few invaders, but they keep reseeding, coming back with a vengeance. What if you tried the "rich topsoil" technique to reclaim your schedule? Rather than constantly trying to get rid of busyness by pulling up one thing at a time, adding enriched nutrients of quiet, solitude,

Perhaps middle age is, or should be, a period of shedding shells.... Perhaps one can at last ... be completely oneself.

—ANNE MORROW
LINDBERGH

98

meditation, and journaling to your life might well be the best possible defense.

Thinking about busyness reminds me of something I wrote in my journal after walking on the beach at Dauphin Island:

> *Sandpiper fast little legs*
> *walk walk walk walk*
> *speed speed speed speed*
> *on the beach*
> *beats my stride*
> *makes me smile*

Even though I have now slowed my pace (for the most part), back in the days of raising children, working, and going to graduate school, at times I looked a lot like this sandpiper. I tried to maintain a connection to nature through my painting, but when I got busy, my awareness lessened. There was a separation in my being. Whenever I stopped to look, smell, and be in nature again, I would feel touched, blessed, and renewed. When I paid attention to nature, I would experience openness, peace, beauty, and the joy of feeling connected to the earth, knowing who I was. But when I drifted back to my demanding life, becoming part of our culture of busyness, I would lose sight of the larger whole—sometimes, even of myself.

Nature has always called me back to myself. When I was twenty-seven and pregnant with my first child, I was inspired by

Taking a solitary walk along a quiet beach, a pond, a woodland path ... allows the busybody chatty mind to disengage with life-buzz and to quiet down.

—PETER LONDON,
*DRAWING CLOSER
TO NATURE*

a neighbor's garden to create a rock garden in my backyard—
though I had never grown anything before. I can remember feeling content and grateful, and I had my first urge to draw in
years. The delicate plants attracted me, and I satisfied myself by
making ink drawings splashed with watercolor. I did not believe
in God at the time, but in retrospect, I can look back and see that
what I would now call Spirit was waking up in me.

Then my daughter, Lindsey, and my son, Jay, were born.
Even though I did not come from a faith perspective, I experienced these births as miraculous. My children delighted me, and
I felt total joy at their existence. Everything about them reawak-
ened me to my senses. They were beautiful and soft, and I loved
to smell their skin. I sensed their goodness—and still do!

The joy in our family, coupled with the supportive love of my
husband, opened me to the possibility of a loving Source, and at
age thirty I came to believe in God. Having a sense of God as creator opened a floodgate of creativity in me. My creative energies
began to flourish, and before long my painting blossomed,
reflecting my interior change.

As I painted, I was attracted to organic forms and the abundant color and light found in nature. Painting was joy for me; I
reveled in what I saw. I lost myself in time, and the days melted
away. I was experiencing *kairos*—the Greek word for the timelessness of God. The scale of the natural forms in my paintings
got larger and larger as the colors got brighter. It was as if I were
beginning to remember my child self. Nothing in my earthly life

*I have come back to my
solitude, my joy, and I
am sure these radiant
skies have much to do
with it.*

—MAY SARTON

had prepared me for this inexpressible sense of belonging with my Creator. I finally felt free.

The idea of *kairos* holds many spiritual possibilities. I think God's timelessness suggests that yesterday, today, and tomorrow are all accessible to us. As a therapist, this idea is especially important to me because I believe that we can go back and heal past pains and reclaim forgotten joys. Perhaps you have childhood wounds that dampen your spirit and hold back your growth. Or you may be tired of feeling tired, of being swamped by life's demands, and you want to put down the burden you've been carrying. Or perhaps, though you are comfortably following your familial or cultural agenda, you still have a nagging sense that "something's missing."

What might open up if you allowed yourself to let go of your busy schedule and gave yourself some *kairos* time? What might happen if you got off the "busy" track and made time in your life for nature, for Spirit, for creativity? What if you were to decide that a simpler life would be richer than the life you now have, crowded with things and commitments? What might you create if you had room in your life to let yourself be present to your true self?

Letting Go of Control

If busyness is a top contender for blocking a free-flowing wellspring, trying to control everything is a close runner-up. I know that before I can let go of something, I often find myself being a

[Our] core is never killed completely. At times it responds to Nature, to beauty, to Life, suddenly aware again of being in the presence of a Mystery … which only has to be glimpsed to renew our spirit and make us feel that life is a supreme gift.

—FREDERICK FRANCK,
THE ZEN OF SEEING

little willful, still desiring to have things *my* way. I have learned to be kind to myself about this willful prelude to letting go; I understand that it is part of my process. Fortunately, I can laugh good-naturedly at my wish to control—even my absurd desire to control the weather.

When we first started SPA Sisters, I had visions of women coming to spend time outdoors in sunny, seventy-degree weather. But I had to quickly let go of that particular wanting. Over the years of SPA Sisters retreats and groups, we seem to have encountered especially difficult weather, ranging from wind and rain and sleet to one-and-a-half feet of snow. And, as you know, I have certainly taken this up with The Weather Maker!

The evening we had the biggest snow during a SPA Sisters Retreat, we had a Wellspring Group down at Island Park on the river near my office. Overhead on the bridge, cars full of angry people trying to get home in the snow were honking and honking at each other. And there we were making snow angels. Then, surprise of all surprises, a young man wearing pink spandex bicycle pants came riding along the snow-covered path on a unicycle! He yelled out, "I bet you're surprised to see me here," and we fell in the snow laughing. We actually had a splendid time. I finally gave up my weather agenda once and for all. What a great way to clear out my wellspring. (By the way, the next retreat was seventy degrees and sunny.)

I can relate to Sandy's story about control:

> There was a time when I tried to control Lake Michigan. We went through a period when the beach was gone. It was eroded, dune grass was taking over, and the lake was filling up. For entire summers there was no place to sit, fish were all over the place, and it was ugly. I would get really anxious

and, against my better judgment, start picking out little pieces of dune grass, trying to create a beach.

Then I would talk to people who had lived there for a long time. I'd say, "What a shame, no beach. Isn't this awful?" They would sit with their backs against the dune and feet in the water (because there was no beach) and reply, "It'll be back." They were totally okay with that. Five years later, we had a wonderful beach. When I look at it now, I think how funny it was that I tired to pick little pieces of grass, as if I could control what was happening.

This was so much bigger than me and people. Along the shore, you can still see the ways people tried to save their beaches, to save the eroded cliffs, and it's almost comical. There are tires, rocks, wood—all kinds of things people have done to try to negotiate and control Lake Michigan. It took only a few years to see what happened to all of the little human schemes. Now the beautiful dune is back, with lots of beach.

Lake Michigan gives me a sense of appreciation for the fact that I'm not in control of the universe. I yield to something bigger than myself, and realize that a much more powerful force than me is in operation. I need to get myself in sync with that and yield to it.

Nature is full of genius, full of the divinity; so that not a snowflake escapes its fashioning hand.

—HENRY DAVID THOREAU

As I go in under the trees, dependably, almost at once, and by nothing I do, things fall into place.... I am less important than I thought, the human race is less important than I thought. I rejoice in that.

—WENDELL BERRY

The truth is that neither Sandy nor I—nor you—have control over natural things like the weather or the beach. I am actually pleased about this. Our culture gives us the idea that we can control everything—and *fast!* I just zipped a few chapters of this book over to my editor and, thirty seconds later, called to see if she had gotten it. We tend to think we make things happen with the push of a button. Yet there is something wonderfully freeing about recognizing that we're not in control of everything, that we don't have to be prepared for all occasions, that we're part of something much greater than we can control with the push of a button.

What things in your life are you trying to keep under control? In what ways does this limit you? What possibilities might open for you if you were to let go of this control? Does the idea excite you? Or scare you? The reality is, sometimes open-ended possibilities can be a bit overwhelming, even a little threatening. So, let's talk about fear for a minute.

Letting Go of Fear

If busyness and control are two big-ticket items on the list for letting go, I think fear completes this daunting trio: fear that there won't be enough, fear that we don't have what it takes, fear of what others will think, fear that we'll be alone. These fears seem to crop up most when we have lost our natural inner resilience, the innate confidence that we were born with, and don't realize we can get it back.

One of the most common, and paralyzing, categories of fear is the fear of what other people think. Public speaking may well be up near the top of this category. I know. The only "D" I received in my life was in a public speaking class in my first year of college. The instructor was very tall and serious and judgmental, and I was terrified. The speaking podium had uneven legs and would click and rock while I spoke and shook with fear. For many years after that class, I avoided public speaking at all costs. My process of letting go of what other people thought began with believing that, if God were truly calling me to speak, then my speaking would reflect on The Artist, not on me. Ever since, I have found the confidence to speak to groups, even large audiences.

My friend Deb's process of letting go of what other people thought began with her diagnosis of cancer. Her story lies in the name she gave herself and her breast cancer-survivor friends: Box Elders. Box elder trees are messy. Many people don't like the way they look because they branch out in different directions on the trunk and appear unkempt. But they are incredibly resilient and tough. Did you know that box elders are the first to come back to life in the forests after a fire? The box elder is a living testament to the fact that beauty does not depend on what people think. The box elder's inner strength and resilience is beauty enough, making it all the more appropriate as a name for Deb and her friends.

That river—who shall say exactly whence it came, and whither it goes? Does aught that flows come from a higher source?

—HENRY DAVID THOREAU

Box Elders

"Messy tree," they say.
"Resilient and strong," I say.
Taking awesome shapes.

I am like the box elder, messy—thought processes.
Resilient and strong—surviving two cancers.
Awesome shapes—fear transformed.

My Friends

I have walked by my three friends
many times
but I did not see them.
I did not see their beauty and courageousness
in the face of their resilience and tenacity.
Struck down, deformed,
by society's standards,
they have reinvented themselves—
another part taking over
for the hurt damaged part
creating a new, unfamiliar yet functioning, flourishing body.

My friends, breast cancer survivors, and I
are like the box elder trees,
with our back and stomach muscles
pulled and stretched into our breasts
to take the place of missing tissue.

Like the box elder trees,
we have survived and
thrived with our resilience
and resolute intention to heal
body, mind, and spirit.

Fear has many shapes and sizes, from the fear of what other people think to the fear of death itself. Even small fears, invasive worries, can send roots into any and every aspect of our lives, rapidly taking over like the worst of the plants that invade the prairie. What does fear look like for you? What does it keep you from doing? How does it keep your wellspring from flowing clearly? Can you imagine what might open up for you if you could let go of fear?

The Other Side of Letting Go

Letting go is part of many religious traditions. For people of Jewish faith, the New Year festival of Rosh Hashanah is a practice of letting go, saying good-bye to the past year and hello to what life can become in the new year. For Muslims, the ritual of fasting during the month of Ramadan begins with the Night of Forgiveness, when arguments of the past are let go. Buddhists believe that the practice of nonattachment greatly reduces suffering because suffering is caused by craving and attachment. A classic Christian teaching of letting go is embodied in Jesus's invitation, "Come to me, all of you who are weary and carry heavy burdens, and I will give you rest. Take my yoke upon you. Let me teach you, because I am humble and gentle at heart, and you will find rest for your souls" (Matthew 11:28–29 NLT).

Yet, when it comes to lessons in letting go, I think my friend Gail might be right when she says that "God's world of nature is the most influential teacher of all." The natural world has a rhythm of letting go. The prairies burn so stronger grasses can grow. The leaves fall to make compost for new growth. Waves wash in and out, creating beautiful patterns in the sand on the beach. Nature is always living, dying, and resurrecting.

One day as I was sitting in my office, I looked out the window and caught a glimpse of this dynamic. Dead berries were still clinging to a tree's branches while new leaves were emerging. I was reminded, once again, that letting go of one part of life or way of being, always opens us up to another. When we let go of what no longer serves us or no longer fits, we make room for something new and alive. Nature has not forgotten this grace-filled process. Letting go can be difficult—even painful—but it can also be freeing. Letting go is a practice of faith, a beginning of hope.

I think of Anne, who participated in a Wellspring Group one autumn during a particularly painful letting-go experience in her life. Here's part of her poem, reflecting both the pain and the promise of letting go:

RED LEAF

Red leaf screaming God's message to me!
Curled and crumbled, violent landing ...

As I watch I begin to see that everything around me—the trees, rocks, river, flowers—everything is simply and profoundly yielded. With that knowing comes a wave of peace.

—PAULA D'ARCY,
GIFT OF THE RED BIRD

Oh, this process of leafing to die,
Letting go dropping, death transformations.

Pry me loose please release me!
This hollow trunk is empty of nurture ...

Let the others hang on and try to stay green,
Lonely brown leaves that still cling in winter.

By then I'll be down the road to greet them,
"Don't be afraid, I didn't know either!"

Red is of stop, red is of danger,
Red is of pain, hurt, and of anger,

Red is a color that takes you where
Red is the color of love and care ...
For red is the passion of "I've been there!"

One of the most difficult letting-go moments we face is the moment of death. I'm grateful that Gail is willing to share some of her thoughts about the death of her daughter and the spiritual journey of passing through this exquisitely painful place to one closer both to her daughter and to God:

Speaking of letting go ... I am standing beside a limb that has been liter-
ally ripped from the tree. This is no small outcropping, but a large, fully

I took grief, loneliness, and confusion to the water and watched it transform over time into gopher snakes and orb weavers, wintercress and thorn apples, red-tailed hawks and white herons, talking leaves and full-bellied moons.

—LORRAINE ANDERSON, *SISTERS OF THE EARTH*

alive branch that was firmly connected to the tree just a day or so ago. This is fresh, this is large, a change that cannot be undone. Unwanted, unwarranted, unfair ... like changes in my life. And yet the tree lives on ... like me. I was forced to let go twelve years ago when my seventeen-year-old daughter Katie died. Each year in this dying season, I must let go once more. It's difficult anew each time. But with the letting go, I move closer to her and closer to my place in this world. For without letting go, I would die in the quagmire of grief. The tree stands firm and tall, reaching to the sky—and so must I.

"Reaching to the sky ...?" Picture yourself doing this. Imagine that you are standing in an open prairie, your body firmly planted on the ground, your hands outstretched, open, not holding on to anything, reaching to the sky. This is the posture of letting go. The vulnerable front and center part of your body is "out there." This is the stance of freedom.

Before we move into an exercise that will help you focus your thoughts about letting go, I want to share one more moment of learning, which came out of a day when I facilitated two Wellspring Groups on letting go:

During the first group, I found—and then lost—a yellow stone I really liked, one that had meaning for me. Later, when I went back to Island Park, rather than being in the present moment, I was trying to find my stone. I was also concerned about the growing dusk. Though I loved the park at dusk, I wondered how the group would work in the dark.

I was so concerned about the women not being able to see, and so focused on finding my stone, that I almost missed the beauty in that moment right in front of me: the setting sun, the sparkling rainbow water, the breeze in the trees, the ducks quacking. Lots of life gets lost looking for what was missing and what is.

When I finally gave up my urge to hang on to my lost stone, and to let go of my worry about other people, I turned and faced an awesome sunset in the present.

Beautiful yellow stone found
And lost—don't look back
You will miss the sunset.

Go forth under the open sky, and listen to Nature's teachings.

—WILLIAM CULLEN BRYANT, THANATOPSIS

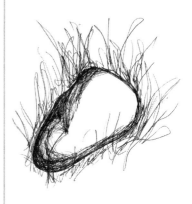

A Clearing Experience

Think of a place in nature that you can get to relatively easily. Dress for the outdoors and collect your journal and whatever pencils, pens, and art supplies you wish.

Once you are outside in your chosen setting, find a place that attracts you and settle in. Look, hear, smell, breathe, and be aware. Then let yourself ease into this meditative exercise: I notice the air, the breeze, the wind, my breath. All speak to me of life, refreshment, renewal, rebirth, even birth. I find myself living in the moment as I concentrate on breathing in, breathing out, letting go of the old in order to create space for the new.

Give yourself some time to consider these questions:

The sky is the daily bread of the eyes.
—RALPH WALDO EMERSON

- What do I need to let go of in order to clear my wellspring?

- What would I like to make space for in my life?

Now look carefully around you. Get up and walk about, if you like, and look for a symbol of letting go that you are drawn to in nature. When you have selected your symbol, find a place to sit quietly and consider:

- What can nature teach me about the natural path of letting go?

Begin to focus your thoughts on the specifics in your life:

- What is one thing I could let go of to begin to make room for something new?

- If I were able to let go of this, how might my life be different? How would letting go of this change the clarity of my wellspring?

Reflect on your thoughts through meditation (just being in the moment, aware of your senses), art, journal writing, poetry, movement, photography—whatever you feel inspired to do.

If you are undertaking this retreat with other women, gather in a circle when you come back together, giving each woman time to share whatever she chooses. Give her your presence with your listening. If she desires a response, share out of your own experience, preferably in nature. Don't judge, advise, or try to fix her. Let go of any inclination to direct or counsel; she has her own path to walk. When everyone has finished, you might want to take time to name the things you are grateful for that have come out of this time together.

Never does nature say one thing and wisdom another.

—JUVENAL, *SATIRES*

113

If you are undertaking these experiences one week at a time, use the following activity for the time in between: Practice letting go by creating room in your life to be in nature for part of each day. Reflect on your time any way you choose. Pay special attention to how it feels to let go of a task or a plan and make time to be outdoors. Notice how this time you create for yourself influences the rest of your day. If you are participating in this exploration with others, share some of your thoughts and feelings about your experience at the start of your next meeting.

SIX

Nurturing

ACCESSING WHAT YOU NEED FOR RESTORATION

What Do You Need?

The music of Hildegard of Bingen has become popular in recent years, especially her medieval hymns, but this amazing twelfth-century woman was much more than a composer. She was also the abbess of a Benedictine convent, a doctor, scientist, writer—and a woman greatly inspired by nature.

I am particularly drawn to a word that Hildegard invented, *viriditas,* which literally means "greening power." She described *viriditas* as "God's freshness that humans receive in their spiritual physical life-forces." For her, the energy of God was "greening power in motion, making all things grow, expand, celebrate." She experienced God as a "breeze that nurtures all things green" and understood salvation, or healing, as "the return of greening power and moistness." Matthew Fox explains in his book *Illuminations of Hildegard of Bingen,* "Hildegard contrasts greening power or wetness with drying up.... A dried-up person and dried-up culture lose their ability to create."

To dry up as a person, to lose the ability to create, to be less than we were created to be—what an apt description of a personal wellspring gone dry. Consider the condition of your wellspring on the wet-to-dry continuum. Where would you place yourself at the moment? Perhaps you have begun to let go of some things that have been blocking your flow of life, energy, and creativity, but you may not have a sense of energy flowing freely yet. It is important to recognize that letting go can create a space that needs to be filled. The question is, filled with *what?* What do you need so your wellspring can flow freely again?

Our culture is quick to bombard us with images of things that can supposedly meet our every need, from instant meals to robot vacuums, from movies on demand to GPS navigation tools. We call this progress, yet from a spiritual standpoint, we seem to be going in reverse, moving further away from what feeds our souls, what nurtures our spirit. We have created the Internet and MP3 players, microwaves and microchips, but somewhere in the process, our creations have begun to take on more importance than Creation—the natural world to which we belong. I think of us as being capable of creating skyscrapers, and then feeling overwhelmed when we look up at the rows of empty windows. As we have gradually shifted from organic to mechanical, from natural to technological, it has become more difficult for us to recognize how out of sync we are with the rest of creation.

The problem is more how to still the soul in the midst of its activities. In fact the problem is how to feed the soul. For it is the spirit of woman that is going dry.

—ANNE MORROW LINDBERGH

In terms of human development, our disconnect from nature has been fairly recent. For thousands of years, people have been living in union with the earth. In *Painters of the Caves,* Patricia Lauber describes the world of the Cro-Magnon Ice Age cave artists as "the world of nature. In it they found food, clothing, and shelter. They observed it closely, so closely that artists working in caves were able to draw from memory." From a psychological standpoint, I think the Cro-Magnons are what ecopsychologist Chellis Glendinning would call "nature-based people": "people who live, or have lived, in direct, unmediated participation with the forces and cycles of the natural world ... people who perceive this Earth to be a sacred place and live accordingly." She describes such people as psychologically open because "they have to be. Their survival in the wilderness depends on a sharp attunement to the world around them ... they must attend to the world with ears, eyes, noses, and skin, alive and alert."

For most of us, it is barely possible to believe that we share these same instincts. Our attunement to the natural world has been buried under technological advancements and fast-paced living, and, for the most part, our relationship with nature has shifted to either detachment or management. But our instincts can be restored, as Glendinning's book title attests: *My Name Is Chellis and I'm in Recovery from Western Civilization.*

Time spent in nature can help us reconnect not only with our sensory instincts, but also with who we truly are and what we need. The prairie, for example, has taught me an important lesson

[A] psychology of the environment would be an expanded psychology of relationship, a conversation or experiencing in the deepest part of our being, of our connection with the Earth as sacred.

—JOHN E. MACK, ECOPSYCHOLOGY

117

The best remedy for those who are afraid, lonely, or unhappy is to go outside, somewhere where they can be quiet, alone with the heavens.... I firmly believe that nature brings solace in all troubles.

—ANNE FRANK

about my need for good boundaries. A mature prairie has a dense matrix of plants that, for the most part, does not allow invaders. The invaders that do get in are not likely to survive the cleansing prairie burns. But there is an exception: the bur oak tree. Because of its tough bark and deep roots, the bur oak can survive the prairie burns and is able to encroach upon prairie grasslands. These oak savannas, as they are called, form transitional areas between the open prairie and the woodland forests. The pioneers who found these patches of trees valued them for their protection, their shade, and their resistance to cold and drought.

For me, as a psychotherapist, the image of the bur oak savanna as transitional space is important. As I am writing this, I realize how tired I am. I have been taking in, and been filled with, many women's stories this week, and it has been an honor to be there to listen. But now I need a period of unbroken solitude. This boundary will give me space and time to reflect. I look out the window, across my neighbors' yards, to the far-off woods that finally break the horizon. I breathe. I start to feel some spaciousness re-enter my being. I need to go outside! I am learning....

I like the way my colleague Marie put it after completing a Wellspring Group: "Who knew that what I have tapped into has been within me all of this time?" This echoes what I think is true for each of us: in our deepest self, we have a recollection of our connection with the earth, and when we immerse ourselves fully in nature, we can access what we truly need for our restoration.

Nature Nurtures

Nature can be harsh. Anyone who has experienced a tornado or midwestern plains blizzard knows that all too well. But nature can also be wonderfully restorative. Spending time in nature can offer us a particularly unique experience of serenity and peace. Perhaps more than any other place or activity, it can offer a calm backdrop for reflection, mirror our inner world, supply wise metaphors, and fill us with a sense of spaciousness and beauty. Unlike our indoor world, nature doesn't encourage us to stay tied up in our thoughts about the past or future; nature draws us into the here-and-now through our senses.

As an artist, I take my senses seriously. I almost always paint outside. I know the joy of really seeing something in the light of the sun, of studying its form and color and texture. I am aware of where light turns to darkness. I notice the smells and sounds that contribute to my sense of the place. The sensual world becomes a part of me and I a part of it.

I think it is precisely this acute awareness of our sensory experience that makes being in nature so nurturing. When we can be fully present to what we see, hear, taste, touch, and feel, the moment becomes rich and nourishing. Sandy talks about one particular outdoor experience that brought her whole family into a nurturing, sacred space:

As the visible world becomes meaningful and vital, we feel it in our bodies. The sensory world thus becomes directly embodied in us; the relationship is visceral, and subjective experience becomes sensuality.

—LAURA SEWALL,
ECOPSYCHOLOGY

You must have been enriched by your solitary walk over the mountains. I suppose that I feel the same awe when on their summits that many do on entering a church.

—HENRY DAVID THOREAU

One time we were in Arizona, where the four corners of the four states come together, and we were heading into the desert. Charlie and I were getting a little nervous, the kids a bit restless. I said, "Charlie, it's getting late, and we are out in this desert. Do we have enough gas? Do we have enough of this and that?" There was not a thing out there, so we kept traveling.

Finally, we came to a reservation. It was a campground owned by Native Americans, and there was just one little spot left. We looked down and there was a canyon below. Above, the sky was changing, and it was the most incredible color I had ever seen: orange and purple and red, dramatic and intense.

The kids had been so restless and tired of driving, and the first thing they wanted to do was go toss a football. But Chad stopped and put the football away, and he started to whisper.

We all sat on the edge of this canyon, and we were just speechless. These two restless kids both kept whispering. This was one of the most incredible experiences ... a spiritual place. To sleep on this very spot seemed almost sacred.

I've always wanted to go back to that place.

Sometimes nurture comes to us unexpectedly, as it did for Sandy's family. But more likely, we need to seek it out, choosing from an array of options that are linked to what our schedules and budgets will allow and where our interests lie: reading, cooking, sewing, gardening, growing house plants, getting a massage or haircut, pressing flowers in a book, lighting candles, making a fire, going to a spa, listening to music, being in solitude—even, for some, cleaning out a closet! It's important, however, to recognize the difference between pampering and nurturing. I think of nurturing as something I can take with me that lasts and has a continuing, satisfying effect on my soul.

One summer thirty-seven years ago, Leon and I camped out in Europe. Late one night, we drove into a campground cut in steps on a huge hill. It was pitch dark, and we could see nothing. Imagine our surprise the next morning when we climbed out of our tent and realized we were facing the sparkling turquoise blue of the Mediterranean Sea—with a camel walking by for good measure. I can still see and feel the joy of that scene. The kind of nurture that nature offers goes deep.

During the years I lived at Prairie Lake, sometimes I would head outside under the guise of painting and end up just staring up at the cerulean blue sky, watching clouds, appreciating the bigness, the brightness, and the openness. My heart felt bigger and stronger, and I was flooded with vast admiration of The Creator. I was filled with gratitude, and I filled my home with vibrant paintings of prairie flowers and landscapes.

You've heard the phrase "nature vs. nurture." My own version is "nature IS nurture." Has that been your experience? What part of nature calls you to come home, to rest, to restoration, to *viriditas,* to yourself? Are you ready to trust what you will find?

The Trust Continuum

Knowing who we are and trusting our intuitive selves is a core piece of getting our needs met because what *we* need is not what someone *else* needs. Each of us is uniquely designed with exactly what we need to live the life we were created for. There is no mistake in our creation. The answers for our lives reside in us just as the code for the tree resides in the seed. As ecopsychologist Michael Cohen so clearly states, "The 'basic' we most need is trust in ourselves, our natural attractions, and our environment ... the most trustable truth in our lives is our immediate experience."

Each of us has different ways of coming to this place of knowing and trusting our instincts and inner wisdom. For Eileen, a simple, direct evening ritual is an important way to understand her response to the day and her needs:

> *I love the sunset. It's like a magic moment. I like to take a little reflective time every day, and the sun closing the day signals that for me. I ask myself, what was my intention for the day, or what were the surprises in my day, or what happened with the people in the day? What was good? What could I make different or better? Where should I have just left it alone or where did I try too hard? It's kind of a spirit connection. I am very interested in what's going on inside me. It matters to be conscious of what's happening, to know where I can shift things.*

Woman's special province is seeing beauty and significance in the small, the close-to-home, and attending to the realm of the heart.

—LORRAINE ANDERSON,
SISTERS OF THE EARTH

Eileen's description reminds me of something Teilhard de Chardin once said: "When I surrender myself to the embrace of the visible and tangible universe, I am able to be in communion with the invisible."

The highest honor we can give our Creator is to trust who we were created to be and to live the life we were made for. But right on the heels of that statement, I want to quickly add one more thought: to limit our scope of trust *only* to ourselves would put severe limits on the greater design. We are part of a grand ecosystem, a larger story than we can know at any given moment.

Nature taught me that truth at the age of eight. My mother had decided to move my brother and me to Denver, in an effort to alleviate her asthma. She also wanted to force my father to get another job away from his beloved Wisconsin farm with which she was so dissatisfied. We moved that summer with the understanding that my father was to follow. He never did. My parents eventually divorced when I was eleven, and I didn't see my father again until long after I was grown.

In Denver, we lived in an apartment surrounded mostly by concrete, and my one nature memory from that year stands out in vivid contrast to the daily landscape. In the alley, a pear-tree branch hung over a fence, and I watched it get heavy with ripe, yellow fruit. I had never seen a pear tree before, and it seemed a sign of hope in a place that felt barren and far away from home and my father. Looking back, I realize that nature was a signpost for me, signaling that there was something more to the story than I could see or understand, even in that impoverished, desperate place. I think this concept touches on the essence of spirituality: that we are called to something beyond ourselves, something that requires trust and faith.

In the midst of a discussion about trusting ourselves, it might seem contradictory to talk about trusting something "beyond us." But I see trust as a continuum that begins with knowing who we are, having faith in who we were created to be, trusting our place in creation, and trusting the one who created us. Trust in ourselves is linked with a greater trust. In my years of practicing therapy, I have seen over and over again that if people do not feel safety and trust within themselves, they find it difficult to have faith in what is beyond.

One summer day when I was leading a Wellspring Group, I felt drawn to a waterfall on the nearby river. As I watched the water, I became aware of a quiet, glassy surface at the top of the falls, just before the water tumbled over into what appeared to be chaos. There was almost a trembling sense of anticipation—not hesitant exactly, but a point where the water seemed to trust that it was okay to "let go" and fall. When the water reached the bottom, it quickly formed a new pattern and flowed on.

As I sat with my thoughts, and prayed, I wrote these words in my journal:

> *The waterfall spills*
> *Trusting the moment*
> *Never waiting.*
>
> *The river below*
> *Continues its flow*
> *Trusting it will*
> *Have what it needs,*
> *A glorious ... neverending dance.*

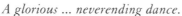

Those who dwell among the beauties and mysteries of the earth are never alone or weary of life.

—RACHEL CARSON

The realization that came to me was this: for the water of my wellspring to flow freely, I need to be like this waterfall, trusting in my Source even when I tumble into new territory—even if my "river" runs dry.

I think this realization I had is close to what Wendell Berry, writer, conservationist, philosopher, and farmer, means when he talks about trust:

> And so my questions do not aspire beyond the earth. They aspire *toward* it and *into* it. Perhaps they aspire *through* it. They are religious because they are asked at the limit of what I know; they acknowledge mystery and honor its presence in the creation; they are spoken in reverence for the order and grace that I see, and that I trust beyond my power to see.

I am intrigued by this idea that we have to go inward to go beyond ourselves. When we move deeply into our creative selves, we tap into something larger than we are, something deeply sacred and profound. Think about the arts for a moment. How is it possible that humans can create symphonies and poems, paintings and books? Surely you've had the experience of being filled with a holy awe at the glorious sounds of an orchestra or the majestic sight of a painting that seemed almost beyond human. I think something similar happens in the natural world. Have you ever stood high up on a mountain and been filled with

I only went out for a walk and finally concluded to stay out till sundown, for going out, I found, was really going in.

—JOHN MUIR

the powerful sense that you are part of something infinitely greater? Or perhaps you've stood under a cold, crystal night sky filled with stars and felt an awed sense of being part of a boundless universe and a humbled sense of being cared for. When we trust who we are as part of creation, we can see ourselves as part of a larger whole.

A Place for Dreaming

If you're from the Midwest, you know what I'm talking about when I say that the sky can feel *huge*! If you've never experienced this vast openness, perhaps you can catch a sense of it in Eileen's memory of crossing the Midwest expanse: "My experience of going off to college was of driving through the cornfields, driving through the countryside. It had a feeling of openness, of opportunity, and of spaciousness. It was the next adventure!"

I've tried to picture the pioneers of our history moving from the protection of the woods, hills, and mountains of the East Coast into the wide open sky and prairie land of the Midwest. No longer sheltered by the shadows of the trees and hills, everything became visible in the intense sunlight, with the flat horizon far in the distance. There was no place to hide.

Maybe seeing the Plains is like seeing an icon: what seems stern and almost empty is merely open, a door into some simple and holy state.

—KATHLEEN NORRIS

In his book *Where the Sky Began: Land of the Tallgrass Prairie,* John Madson reminds us that these first families who arrived on the prairies were used to sun that rose and set through trees. Going back eight generations, they had probably never seen a sunset on an unbroken horizon. Now "they stood under an infinite vault of sky in a world reduced to three immensities: the grass below, the sky above, and the single horizon beyond."

When I first moved out to the prairie from the tree-shaded suburban area where I had lived for twenty-five years, I felt naked in the face of the big sky. I could not get away from it. Everywhere I looked was a 360-degree expanse. When there was a thunderstorm, I could see "trees" of lightning crashing down from every direction. I knew my vulnerability. I could not hide. I was used to being hemmed in by houses; out on the prairie, I had no false protection of close buildings and trees. I was used to depending on close, beloved, nurturing friends; out on the prairie, it was just me and the open sky.

Yet on sunny days, when white puffy clouds wafted by, I began to feel the joy of the prairie. At night, I felt like one of the jewels in the pitch-black, star-filled heavens. In storms, I felt fearfully part of the wind pulling on the house, with nothing in the way to stop it. I reverenced rainbows and double rainbows, unbroken from one end to the other. There was nothing false— either to protect me or to prevent me from seeing new possibilities. In a landscape with no barriers, God seemed much bigger.

This sense of openness brought me to a larger version of my own life. Maybe that is why I identify so closely with Sandy's

I remember what the city has to offer ... a clatter of quickening stimulus like a rush from strong drugs that leaves you drained. I remember how you bide your time in the city, and think, if you stop to think, "next year ... I'll start living."

—ANNIE DILLARD

description of her similar experience with the expanse of Lake Michigan:

> *When you get to the sands of the beach, you look out on this limitless horizon that has no land on the other side. That has become my space, my place to meditate and get in touch with my own spirit. That's where I'm drawn for sustenance, to nourish my spirit.*
>
> *There's something about the fact that there's no horizon on the other side that brings me into infinity; it takes me out of my boundaries. I am so minute in terms of infinity, and yet—and yet—I am so affirmed by God in my little space on the beach.*

Nature is always hinting at us. It hints over and over again. And suddenly we take the hint.

—Robert Frost

Being open puts us in a state of both vulnerability and possibility. When we open ourselves to the water, to the sky, to the Creator, we are letting go of old ways of seeing things, of old patterns that have cramped our lives. This can be incredibly freeing, charging us with the exhilaration of both fear and joy. What wild storms might come racing across the open space? What dazzling night-sky beauty awaits behind the setting sun? What glorious sunrises might emerge at dawn?

The best response I can give is this: daring to be open is the only way to access the fullness and possibility of life. Pam captures this beautifully in her journal entry about a nature walk she took at a time in her life when she was letting go of a career, and space was opening up for her:

128

Today is very cold. In my walk by the river, I first went to stand by the waterfall—watching the power of moving water and the churning froth it created. Beautiful as this was, it wasn't reaching what was at my inner core.

Seeking shelter from the wind, I headed under the bridge. It didn't help much to make me feel warmer, and there was nothing speaking to me there, so I edged around it to stand by the side of the river. I looked at a tall, stalky plant, unbelieving at first. I couldn't quite register what I was looking at, but there it was ... a tattered cornstalk! How had it come to grow in the river?

Thinking it over, I realized that the drought of the past summer had created a sort of "open space," a narrow strip of beach in the place where water normally would have been. Somehow, a kernel of corn had found its way there and rooted in the moist soil. It had entered that open space with a new kind of life.

This echoes what is happening with me. Since letting go of my job, I feel free. I am like that kernel of corn finding life in a newly opened space.

There's one more thing to mention about being open to new possibilities: they may not always be where or what you expected. As Annie Dillard put it in *Pilgrim at Tinker Creek*, "There are lots of things to see, unwrapped gifts and free surprises. The world is fairly studded and strewn with pennies cast broadside from a generous hand."

Patty received one of these "unwrapped gifts" in an experience she had with her husband, Gregg, shortly before he was diagnosed with cancer. They had gone to the beach on Lake Michigan near Sandy's house. The weather was stormy and drizzling and the wind had picked up, but they really wanted to go for a swim, so in they went.

Patty's vivid memory of that day is of strong waves, cold water—and laughing and laughing.

At the time, they did not know that Gregg's life was becoming short. As Patty describes it, "I remember being with Gregg and really feeling a connection to him, a connection to nature, and a connection to life and everything around me."

If trust is the basic seed of beginnings, then connection is the energizing growth, and "free surprises," as Annie Dillard puts it, are the quintessential bloom. The next time you step outside, pay attention to what you see and hear and feel. Notice how nature nurtures. Most of all, be open to nature's surprises. When you open the door to the outdoor world, you open the door to Spirit, to possibilities, to life.

When people make thoughtful contact with nature, they become more sensitive to life.... Their spiritual relationship with the outdoors empowers and guides them. Natural areas nurture them.

—MICHAEL COHEN,
RECONNECTING WITH NATURE

A Nurturing Experience

Get dressed in comfortable outdoor clothing and gather your journal, crayons, pens, pencils, and anything else you would like to use to express yourself. Go outside and look for an area where you can sit down and spend some time being aware of your breath—and just *being*.

When you find an area you are drawn to, settle in and begin this meditative exercise: *"It is in the darkness that we find the light"* (Meister Eckhart). Sometimes it is necessary to go into the darkness to see the light. In the darkness, I can pay attention to the shadows, I can find solitude. I can pay attention to what is happening around me in a different way. I can hear the sounds of nature, the scent of the earth and its plants, the feel of the ground beneath me. The darkness inspires me to think about the world and my place in it.

As you stay with this idea of darkness, be especially aware of your senses as you consider each of these questions:

- What is it about being in this place in nature that feels nourishing and gives life to my spirit?

- How does being in this space help me come to a better understanding of what I need to do in order to replenish my wellspring?

Bread feeds the body, indeed, but flowers feed also the soul.

— Qur'an

131

• What are the specific elements in this space that meet my needs?

Look around you for a metaphor in nature that shows a need being met naturally. What might this metaphor suggest about meeting your need?

Reflect on your experience through meditation (just being in the moment, aware of your senses), art, journal writing, poetry, movement, photography—whatever comes naturally to you.

If you are undertaking this retreat with other women, gather in a circle when you come back together and allow each woman to share what she wishes about what she has learned. Receive her just as she is, without judgment or advice. As you are trying to trust yourself, give her the gift of your trust. When everyone has finished, you might want to take time to name the things you are grateful for that have come out of this time together.

If you are undertaking these experiences one week at a time, use the following activity for the time in between: find a place in nature that you are drawn to in the area where you live. Reflect on how this natural environment is a restorative, nurturing place for your spirit. If you are doing this exploration with others, share some of your reflections at the start of your next meeting.

SEVEN

Belonging

CREATING INNER HARMONY

A Sense of Harmony

Whenever I think of the prairie, I visualize completeness. The prairie is my picture of harmony. It is a self-sustaining community of living creatures relating to one another in a constantly changing environment. Large animals such as deer and, further west, bison, are part of this amazingly complex but efficient ecosystem. Birds build their nests and raise their young. I once saw a bird's nest woven around the stalks of a compass plant—it was a sight to behold, the creation of a master weaver! Gophers burrow underground and mice nest near the ground. All are able to find their way through the grass jungle. Insects provide food and find food themselves. In midwestern prairies you might see pheasants, badgers, buffalo, elk, white-tailed deer, monarch butterflies, rabbits, and a wide variety of beautiful native prairie flowers and grasses. It is a complete yet diverse

Beauty of earth and sea and air meant more to me. I was in harmony with it, melted into the universe, lost in it, as one is lost in a canticle of praise, swelling from an unknown crowd in a cathedral.

—ANNE MORROW
LINDBERGH

ecosystem teaming with life and vitality, and these apparently divergent elements come together as a harmonious whole.

Harmony is not something we often experience in our high-tech world. As our culture has become more "civilized," we seem to have sacrificed harmony for efficiency and productivity. We seem to have forgotten that we are creatures that once were in perfect sync with nature's rhythms. Yet harmony is something we long for and try to recreate.

Webster's defines *harmony* as "an internal calm; tranquility." Seeking refuge from our pressured lifestyles, we have become seekers of this elusive treasure. Will a latte do it? Maybe a pedicure or some other service will calm us. Actually, I like lattes and pedicures, but these things do not bring internal harmony. Ecopsychologist Chellis Glendinning captures the essence of our search in these words: "As our lives are upset by more personal crises and the earth is marred by more ecological disasters, we find our quiet wonderings growing, taking on greater urgency, becoming loud and pressing questions. Why don't we feel well? Why is there so much fear? Why are life-affirming experiences and resources so elusive for us?"

We know that we need to stop rushing around, we know that we need a sanctuary, but the quest for peace and quiet seems elusive, if not impossible. Who has the time and space for *harmony*?

Yet we each have within our reach, every day, a phenomenal tool to facilitate our return to harmonious living: creation. Every aspect of the natural world reflects the wholeness of The Creator, the harmony of life. The Artist is visible in the artwork. In this physical reflection, we can begin to see ourselves and our place in the harmonious whole.

If you're thinking, "But I'm surrounded by skyscrapers.... I see only concrete," my reply is, "Look up; the sky is different every day. Do you have a park nearby? I spent one of the best days of my life at Central Park in New York City." Even if you can only find a leaf to look at or a stone to touch, every touch of nature, no matter how small, has much to teach about harmony. *Immersion* in nature is not as important as *attention* to nature.

Harmony awaits just outside the door, in a yard or a park, at the edge of a river or down a path, in a cloud or in a tree. Nature is typically a harmonious, serene, and peaceful place, so each time we make a conscious choice to spend time outdoors, we give ourselves a chance to experience a harmonious balance. Each time we let ourselves just *be* in nature, we create a possibility for serenity to seep into us. I love the way Michael Cohen puts it in *Reconnecting with Nature:* "At any given moment we can choose to reconnect with nature and regain the comfort of being in equilibrium."

The word *equilibrium* is important here because there are certainly times when nature goes off on a rampage and becomes hardly serene. Yet if we think of harmony as the "right and desirable relationship of parts to a whole," as the *Encarta Encyclopedia* defines it, we begin to grasp the idea that harmony is more than "peace and quiet"; it is a beautiful working

One touch of nature makes the whole world kin.

—WILLIAM SHAKESPEARE

135

together, a sense of rightness, a feeling of unity and completeness. Every part matters and every part contributes to the whole.

One of the basic premises of ecopsychology is that, although we are shaped by our modern social world, we can be inspired and comforted by the natural world because that is our origin. Not only do we depend on nature for our physical sustenance, we need it for our mental health as well. Our relationship with the earth is crucial to our sense of harmony. Yet the word more likely to describe our modern relationship with nature is *manipulation,* not *harmonization.* We know how to dam rivers, genetically modify corn, control insects with chemicals—even how to clone animals. But in the process of garnering this control, we've severed our life-giving relationship with creation. We do not have "the comfort of being in equilibrium" with our planet. Listen to these powerful words from ecopsychologist Mary Gomes in *Ecopsychology: Restoring the Earth, Healing the Mind:*

> We regard [the earth] as a thing, a big thing, an object to be owned, mined, fenced, guarded, stripped, built upon, dammed, plowed, burned, blasted, bulldozed, and melted to serve the material needs and desires of the human species.... This attitude contrasts dramatically with the ... reverential relationship with nature that is reflected in the words of Native American leaders, who recognize

What a thing it is to sit absolutely alone, in the forest, at night, cherished by ... the most comforting speech in the world, the talk that rain makes by itself all over the ridges, and the talk of the watercourses everywhere in the hollows.

—THOMAS MERTON

our complete interdependence with the Earth and the need to live in balance and harmony with nature.

Even though the idea of harmony with nature may seem elusive on a day-to-day basis, most of us experience this sense of harmony as children. I have a vivid childhood memory of raspberry picking with my family in northern Wisconsin. I still have the visual images, the tastes, the feeling of the textures and the smells of that day over five decades ago. I can still picture the blue sky, the shining sun; I see myself in a sweet-smelling meadow with fluffy green grass and "cow pies" (which are somehow positive). I have a can with a string attached hanging around my neck. After picking several of the succulent, ripe red berries and dropping them in the can, I retrieve them and push them into my mouth. I can still smell and taste the sweetness. I can feel their plump, juicy texture in my mouth. I have loved raspberries ever since.

The problem is, even though we may have experienced this sense of harmony—if only briefly—we have trouble hanging on to it or reproducing it as adults. The good news is, each time we return to nature, we place ourselves in a position to re-access the harmony we once knew; we open a way to experience harmony within ourselves and with our world. But there is one catch: we run into problems when our idea of harmony and nature's version aren't exactly the same.

Living in balance and harmony with nature sounds lovely—especially if scenes of warm days, serene beaches, and golden sunsets come to mind. But nature is wonderfully wild and unpredictable, and our idea of harmony may need some adjustment. When Gail attended a six-week Wellspring Group, she happened to come at a time when the weather was consistently difficult—strong winds, unseasonable cold, gray skies, and driving rain. Her experience of harmony came anyway:

I stand beneath the umbrella of the willow tree. It reaches out over the river in a graceful arch. It shows me much more grace than I could ever return. Together, the dead branches and the live green branches form this protective spot for me. The soft trickle of the rain that manages to get through the branches is a soothing sound. It even mingles well with the white noise of the traffic that is just over my shoulder. In harmony, both natural and human sounds soothe my caustic mood. The raindrops fall into the river, filling its banks and moving it ever forward. I want to come into harmony with this ever-present thing called weather. I want to move with it and embrace it. As the river receives the gift of the skies, so will I. I huddle close to the trunk of this wizened tree and take a lesson from it. Be still. Stop. Listen. Smell. Taste. Touch. Harmonize. Just harmonize.

A Sense of Connection

It is often said that we live in an age of disconnect. We lament the disconnect between generations, the disconnect between genders, the disconnect within families, the disconnect between our institutional religions and our spiritual hunger. And it almost goes without saying that we are disconnected from nature much of the time. When we run into the grocery store to pick up something for dinner, the farm that grew the wheat or raised the chicken is hardly at the forefront of our thoughts. We seldom stop to think about where our food and water come from, let alone where it (and all the packaging it comes in) will end up. We have efficiently isolated ourselves from our sources of physical sustenance, effectively denying our connection with nature.

For indigenous peoples all over the world, the relationship to nature is intrinsic to living because they depend on nature for their survival. They also experience their connection with nature as inseparable from their spirituality. Through nature, they understand their God as the source of all life and they share this dependence on God-given elements with all living things— plants, trees, animals. They respond to creation much as Meister Eckhart did, as "a revelation of God, a home for God and a Temple for God ... an overflow of the beauty that God is."

People of all traditions find the sacred in the natural world. According to Hindu thought, there is no separation between the Divine and the world of nature. The Buddha taught the importance of living in harmony with the natural world and appreciating our interconnectedness. Followers of Islam believe that study of the visible cosmos can reveal the spiritual world beyond it. Central to Jewish thought is the belief that all creation is sacred. The Christian Gospels tell us that Jesus would often slip away to the wilderness to pray. The first Christian monks moved to the desert in the fourth and fifth centuries to seek God. In his famous "Canticle to the Sun," Saint Francis, who has been named the patron saint of ecology because of his deep connection to nature, described himself as a brother to the sun and moon, wind and air, birds and animals. He could not envision journeying toward God apart from the rest of the family of creation. The twentieth-century Trappist monk Thomas Merton also understood our profound connection with nature. He believed

In our souls and hearts all of us retain a faint but compelling memory of our spiritual connection with the Earth ... but after many years of being too civilized, few can lock onto the signal.

—PHILIP CHARD,
THE HEALING EARTH

that to be alienated from the natural world is to be alienated from our deepest self—and from God.

In the foreword to *When the Trees Say Nothing: Writings on Nature by Thomas Merton,* Thomas Berry underscores the gift of the Sacred through nature:

> We find ourselves in a critical moment when [we] need to awaken again to the natural world as a primary manifestation of the divine ... the very nature and purpose of the human is to experience this intimate presence that comes to us through natural phenomena.... Everywhere we find ourselves invaded by the world of the sacred.

The idea that our connection with the earth connects us with the holy is a compelling concept. I have a friend, John Lionberger, who wrote a book called *Renewal in the Wilderness: A Spiritual Guide to Connecting with God in the Natural World* (SkyLight Paths) about the trips he leads to bring people back to nature. John believes that "in our isolation from nature, we have lost that direct, personal connection to the holy." Every time he makes a presentation about his trips, he sees the visible evidence of our universal longing: "At the end of virtually every talk, people approach me with eyes that are bright with reminiscence. They tell me stories of how alive they felt in their childhood when they were outside, in nature, often on camping trips.... Their hunger

I cannot have enough of the hours of silence when nothing happens. When the clouds go by. When the trees say nothing. When the birds sing. I am completely addicted to the realization that just being there is enough.

—THOMAS MERTON

for a deeper spiritual connection is written on their faces and in the wistfulness of their eyes."

Though we may not have the language to describe it, we somehow grasp, as poet and essayist Kathleen Norris has said of her ancestral home in South Dakota, that "nature ... can indeed be an experience of the holy."

The German theologian and philosopher Friedrich Schleiermacher proposed that what he called "religiousness" is primarily a matter of intuitive feeling, an immediate experience, a sense of the infinite, that is prior to language. This is the uncontaminated, pure experience that Patty describes in a memory of playing as a very young child: "There was a little school down the street with big fields of grass and trees. I remember feeling a connection to those trees, like they were almost part of me, of my life. I knew their little nooks and crannies. We'd play there all the time. It was a spiritual place for me."

Nature continues to be an important companion for Patty; it is woven into her relationships with other people. In an uncomplicated time before her husband, Gregg, was diagnosed with cancer, they shared an intimate moment of connection with nature, with God, and with each other:

> *I remember being on a hiking trip with Gregg in Starved Rock State Park in Illinois. Out there hiking, I felt so close to God and so close to nature. I was just following Gregg's trail, which was nice*

When we try to pick out anything by itself, we find it hitched to everything else in the Universe.

—JOHN MUIR

because then I didn't have to think about which way to go and I could sort of get into a meditative state.

All of a sudden, a couple of deer were right in front of us. I didn't want them to be afraid and run away because they were so beautiful, so I just started talking sweetly to them: "Oh, it's a beautiful day out. It must be so nice to walk through these forests." Pretty soon I could tell their ears were pointed toward me and they were listening. Gregg was very excited to see the deer, too, and we both stood really still. Just like that, in the middle of the forest, we had this connection.

On what would be the last trip that Patty and Gregg had before he died, they went to Little Marais, Minnesota, and stayed in a cabin on Lake Superior:

We had been going up to Lake Superior for many years, and I always looked for the Northern Lights, but I never got to see them. Sometimes, I would set my alarm to wake me in the middle of the night, and I would go outside for an hour, hoping. On this trip, we made a little campfire on the beach every night. At the time, we didn't know Gregg had cancer, so everything was wonderful. We were just lying back, talking, and letting the fire cool. We were having a great time in this total nature; we could see all the stars, and here we were on the lake, watching this beautiful fire die down. All of a sudden the sky was filled with Northern Lights. I had never seen such a show, and we lay out there on the sand for hours.

In Northern Minnesota at that time of year, the sun doesn't set until very late and the sun comes up very early in the morning, so there are only

a few hours of darkness. We stayed until sunrise, and then we went back
up into the cottage. Neither one of us got any sleep that night. It was one
of our last nights together on that trip, and our last summer vacation
together. To have that experience with Gregg felt like a gift from God.

In my work with SPA Sisters, I have been privileged to hear many such powerful stories about women's connections with nature. Some are vivid memories from childhood. Others are oriented to the present moment but described in a childlike, sensate way. Over and over again, I hear women say that when they reconnect with nature, they not only access a very alive part of themselves, but they also experience a renewed awareness of their connection to other people and to their Creator.

As you read this vignette of a life-giving gift my colleague Marie received from her father, let yourself feel this childhood moment of awe in her physical and spiritual connection:

I was nearly four years old, living on the edge of the city of Seattle, splash-
ing contentedly in my nightly summer bath. Unknown to me, the whole
neighborhood had been drawn outside to cast their eyes to the night skies as
the modern wonder of a "man-made" satellite passed overhead. My father
shifted his gaze around the crowd gathered on our less-wooded front lawn,
which allowed the best vantage point in this hilly neighborhood. Realizing
that his third of four children was not present, he dashed into the house,
grabbed a big fluffy bath towel, snatched me from the water and, swad-
dling me, held me tight as he dashed back out into the night.

There, to my wonder, was a quiet crowd with their eyes lifted to the dome
of the night sky. I, naturally, followed their gaze, and, not comprehending

this "man-made" space-age wonder that held their attention, all I saw was the bowl of thousands of stars piercing the darkness. In my father's arms I saw, for the first time in my young life, the celestial lightshow of sparkling stars. I can still feel my father's breath on my cheek as I stretched my neck as far back as it would arch. I still feel the safety of his embrace in spite of my shivers under the encircling towel. From that moment I have associated the canopy of stars with the attentions of a father, and a Father Creator.

It's time. Time to reconnect with nature, not by seeing it through a window but by being *in* it. Not by writing or talking about how amazing nature is but by drinking in its quiet solitude. It is one thing to know, intellectually, that the sacred is present in creation. It is another to experience it in your heart, to feel it at the deepest level of your being.

A Sense of Home

Every year, the Maryland Center for Agro-Ecology cosponsors a lecture series called "Journeys Home" and invites speakers to explore our identity with nature. In one lecture, Frederick Kirschenmann posed the question, "What does it mean to be at home?"

What nature creates has eternity in it.

—Isaac Bashevis Singer

His answer began simply enough: "For most of us, being at home simply means being in an apartment or house or condo where we usually sleep and where we, once in a while, eat meals with our family members or watch television. Home for us is mostly an enclosure which protects us from the rest of the world around us—usually with a little help from security personnel and technology."

Perhaps his most important statement about being "at home" was his assertion that we are connected to everything in the cosmos. This is akin to what cosmologist Brian Swimme talks about in his video series *Canticle to the Cosmos:* that not only are we all part of the same numinous energy, but our relationship with the cosmos inspires great joy. I think this is a little of what Pam tapped into during one Wellspring Group:

> *As I enter the magical outdoors—transformed by the snow falling quickly before my eyes—I am drawn down the block. I need to feel like I am in the woods, and only a block away is a corner lot, a mini-forest.*
>
> *Dried red berries cling to bare, thorny branches. Trees are elegant in their stripped-down winter attire. Thick and thin, they gracefully bend toward and away from one another, reminding me of Kahlil Gibran's lovely poetry in* The Prophet, *where he voices the idea of allowing spaces in togetherness.*
>
> *I am part of this universal dance, whether I am conscious of it or not. Only feet away are noisy cars and trucks, with snowplows scraping along, but in this small wooded lot, quiet reigns.*
>
> *I can choose the noise and distraction, or this quiet place where there is beauty and harmony. That decision is always mine.*
>
> *In walking back to the meeting room, my earlier footsteps are already filling in with fresh snow. Soon, there will be no trace of them, but I carry*

Once we begin to feel at home in the woods and waters, mountains, deserts, prairies, and skies, then we always have a sanctuary.

—PHILLIP CHARD,
THE HEALING EARTH

with me the knowledge that I've been transformed in spirit by my brief time in this gentle place.

It's time to come home to the "universal dance" we are already part of. Though our knowledge of nature is greater than that of any previous generation, we seem to be less at home in the natural world than ever before. It's time to walk away from the computer, the TV, the to-do list and literally walk on the earth.

Whenever I spend time in nature, I have a sense of coming home. It wasn't always like that for me. When I first started going out into nature as an adult, I actually felt pretty uncomfortable. With the exception of brief awarenesses of nature moments, the distress of my childhood had truly grabbed my attention away from any sort of natural sanctuary. I bumbled my way back unintentionally.

When we moved to Prairie Lake, I had planned to run retreats to nourish others, not myself. What I hadn't accounted for was the loneliness I brought with me that I had been too busy to notice before. The problem was, on that much land out in the middle of nowhere, there was nothing else to do but go outside. As I began spending longer periods of time outdoors, I started to feel part of nature. My senses were waking up. I noticed how fresh the air smelled—unless I was visiting the hog farm down the street! The lake showed me a different face every day. The woods sprouted wildflowers I hadn't seen or smelled since childhood. And to hide in the woods under a bed of leaves, *ahhhh* ...

this was one of my favorites. I also loved the sun warming my face and body. On my days off, I would slather on suntan lotion and zoom out the door to paint. Since there was no one else around, I didn't even think about putting on makeup or care if my clothes matched. It was great to abandon myself to that natural place. I felt very free. I had found peace, a haven. I belonged.

I began to truly grasp that nature is with me wherever I go. Nine years after we moved to Prairie Lake, the land around it began to be built up with housing developments, and we decided it was time to leave. At first I felt sad and disappointed, but then I realized that I didn't have to stay at Prairie Lake to be in nature. Nature is *everywhere;* I didn't need to own it. (But it is nice to know that the people who now live at Prairie Lake have kept the prairie beautiful and blooming.) I now live in the country on a one-and-a-half-acre lot backed by many acres of woods. I have created a simple Japanese garden on the hill in back of my home. My hands are constantly beat up from my continuing urge to dig in the dirt and see what grows. I know and care for each plant and tree. Most every day, I spend some time in this sheltered space of my backyard, gazing sometimes at the sky bright with sunshine, other days, at clouds dark gray and brooding. I am presented with a new landscape, painted by The Artist, every day. I identify with the hawks slowly gliding over head, their movement looking smooth and effortless.

Desert wisdom allows you to be at home wherever you are.

—KATHLEEN NORRIS

147

One morning the sun shone so brightly that each tree in the forest beyond the yard glistened gold, and I saw a thoroughly golden breasted hawk perched on the highest branch. This was one of those "forever" moments I still have with me. I felt aware of all my senses and was filled with appreciation for "what is." I echoed the divine pronouncement in the beginning of Genesis: "It is very good." I felt part of it all ... blessed. I was home.

Whenever I walk in the garden or in the woods behind my house, my sensory alertness almost matches that of my child self. It is this being fully present that opens me to the sacred connection in nature. This is one of nature's most precious gifts: when we are present, alive, and conscious of our surroundings, not stuck in the past or roaming the future, we can have a profound sense of peace with the whole. We don't need to wait until every circumstance is "right"—or we might be waiting for a long time! As Eileen puts it, "It's not about controlling everything, trying to get the outcome to be what you want it to be. Just put yourself on the path and let it be, let it happen."

In the best sense, nature is like a dance where every one of us—every leaf, flower, and creature—has a part that fits. Perhaps the only—and best—thing we can do is to be present to the dance. This was my prayer in a journal entry from one Wellspring Group:

Wonder is everywhere. Please open my eyes, God, to herons, spiderwebs, and shimmering water. Help me to be present in this moment and let all else fall away.

To forget how to dig the earth and to tend the soil is to forget ourselves.

—MAHATMA GANDHI

Everything in the universe has rhythm. Everything dances.

—MAYA ANGELOU

Beautiful heron
Surprise
As I walk the bridge.

The next moment
A hawk soars
Into my view
I am here.

Dr. Rachel Naomi Remen, pioneer of the holistic health movement and author of *Kitchen Table Wisdom,* said something quite profound in an address she gave to a psychology convocation. She described the recovery of the sacred not as finding "something more" or even "fixing yourself," but rather as remembering something you've forgotten, something you may have hidden from yourself.

Over many years I taught masters- and doctoral-level students and engaged in untold discussions of psychological theory, but I find myself pulling away from the professional words and clinical terminology. I think of my job as creating a safe space for people to remember what they have forgotten about themselves. I believe good psychology and good theology go together.

Are you ready to come home, to come back to what you've forgotten or to find what has gotten lost? Are you ready to uncover or rediscover the innate wholeness in the world and in yourself? Come home to your authentic core, to experience the fullness of who you were created to be, both personally and spiritually. Come home to harmony.

A Belonging Experience

Gather up your outdoor clothing, your journal, pens, pencils, and whatever other art materials appeal to you. Find a place outside that feels good to you. Get comfortable and allow yourself to spend some time becoming aware of your breath as you breathe slowly, in and out ... in and out. Then move into this meditative exercise: I spend time listening to myself and the world around me. I begin to understand that everything in life has a purpose. Being outside in nature, I can experience harmony. As I allow myself to have this experience, I am encouraged to find a way to bring it into my life. Harmony is reflected in nature. I am part of nature.

Now look around for a special spot where you might feel completely at home in nature, or for a natural object that you feel a special kinship with. Take time to really experience and be part of the harmony of this place or this object. Move your body and settle into the space, or touch, smell, taste, and thoroughly look at the object. Pay attention to all of your senses and how they are affected by being outside. Notice all of the aspects of your chosen place or object that are in harmony with one another. Reflect on what it is like to feel peaceful and just *be*.

Consider these questions:

- Am I "at home" with a clear wellspring?

A life in harmony with nature ... will purge the eyes to understanding her text.

—RALPH WALDO EMERSON

- How can I experience more harmony in my daily life?

Look carefully around you once more. This time select something in nature that can be a metaphor for the harmony you want in your life. Reflect on your metaphor through meditation (just being in the moment aware of your senses), art, journal writing, poetry, collection, movement, photography—whatever you feel moved to do.

If you are undertaking this retreat with other women, gather in a circle when you come back together and take plenty of time for each woman to share whatever she wants to. Thoroughly listen to each woman, enjoying her presence and the life that is in her. Make no effort to change her, judge her, or give her advice. Just be with her. It is for her to make choices and live her life. Trust her. Trust yourself. When everyone has finished, you might want to take time to name the things you are grateful for that have come out of this time together.

If you are undertaking these experiences one week at a time, use the following activity for the time in between: Take time this week to get "in sync" with the harmonious rhythms of nature. Spend time just *being* in a natural place where you feel a sense of belonging. Be aware of your senses. Reflect on your connection in nature. If you are participating in this exploration with others, share some of your experiences at the start of your next meeting.

It is a wholesome and necessary thing for us to turn again to the earth and in the contemplation of her beauties to know of wonder and humility.

—RACHEL CARSON

EIGHT
Balancing

REACHING OUT AND REPLENISHING

First Wisdom: Conservation

There is a wonderful symbol of balance in the prairie flower called the cup plant. A close relative of the compass plant, it has a root system deeper than the plant is tall. Like the compass plant, the cup plant also has large, tough leaves and yellow flowers. Even in the midst of a hot, arid summer, it looks fresh and perky. Apparently, it knows how to get what it needs for itself. The cup plant has many strong, stalky, hairy, square stems reaching up, with the large leaves growing in pairs opposite one another.

This is where the plant gets really interesting. The leaf pairs are joined at the bottom at the same place on the stem, forming cups. These cups hold water from rain, and when the summer gets dry, birds come by for a drink. It makes me think of a line from Proverbs: "Like cold water to a weary soul" (25:25 NIV). It

Upon emergence from wilderness we are confronted with our inconsistencies and notice more than ever before how drastically out of balance we live.

—STEVEN HARPER,
ECOPSYCHOLOGY

amazes me that this plant not only takes care of itself in a drought, but also has the ability to share its reservoirs of water with the birds. Talk about a living lesson! I think the cup plant has much to teach us about the balance between caring for ourselves and caring for others.

If you were to list what a spiritual life would include, helping others would surely be somewhere near the top of the list. Yet if we take the Proverbs admonition to "guard your heart, for it is the wellspring of life" seriously, where does that leave us? How do we help others and guard our wellspring at the same time? Taking care of ourselves can be a challenge when we're confronted with the needs of our jobs and our families, our schools and our churches, our communities and our planet. Too often our personal needs don't even make the list, or if they do, they're somewhere near the bottom of the priorities. "There just isn't enough time!" we argue.

It's time for us to think *seriously* about balance. We typically use the word *balance* in a cavalier fashion: I need to get my tires rebalanced, I've got to balance my bank account, I'd like to start eating a more balanced diet. But the kind of balance I'm talking about goes much deeper. This balance is a considered, thoughtful counteraction to what the Hopis call *koyaanisqatsi*. You might recognize this term from the title of the 1982 film classic; it means "life out of balance; a state of life that calls for another way of living."

Does that description fit your life in any way? When was the last time you said to yourself, "There's got to be another way!" as you tried to run errands, return phone calls, check e-mails, make dinner, do the laundry. What about the promises you've made to yourself that you *will* take a break for yourself when … but the "when" never arrives.

In nature, if things get out of balance, they typically die. For instance, if I water my plants too much, or not enough, the lack of balance can be fatal. Too little or too much—even of a good thing!—can stifle a life. I think of the various plants in my house. The peace lily really likes water. If I forget to water it, it certainly lets me know. It slumps over and folds into itself. But as soon as I respond, it perks right back up. Then there are my orchids. Because of their beautiful, long-lasting cascades of flowers, you might think they need a lot of water to keep the show going. This is not true. These orchids require very little water and care to enhance their lives, and I would hurt, maybe even kill them, with over-watering.

Just as each plant species has different needs for its growth, so, too, does each of us have different needs at different times. The key is to find the balance that works for us. Just as nature honors a balance between wet and dry, hot and cold, predator and prey, night and day, asleep and awake, it is vital to our mental, physical, and spiritual health that we find the balance that is best for our lives. And since nature is such an expert, what better teacher could we have?

The midwestern prairies provide a mini-lesson—or, more accurately, given the size of the prairie, a magnified lesson—on the subject of balance. When it comes to water needs, most of the prairie grasses and native wildflowers blossom or grow dormant depending on the available moisture. When there is plenty of rain, they produce abundant foliage and flowers. When there is a drought, they rely on their

I think of the trees and how simply they let go, let fall the riches of a season, how without grief (it seems) they can let go of and go deep into their roots for renewal and sleep.

—MAY SARTON

extensive underground root networks to seek out moisture, and they remain in a semi-dormant state to conserve their resources.

This is nature's first wisdom: when you are dry, you need to make it a priority to conserve your resources, to take care of yourself. Another way of saying it is: be aware of your limits. You can't keep blooming, expending your energy all over the place without replenishing, or there will be nothing left. When you feel dry, it's time for some dormancy—a little nesting, resting, meditating, walking, reflecting, praying, drawing, and writing.

Even though summer is my favorite season, I am thankful to live in a climate where plants go dormant. If I lived in year-round warmth and sunshine, I would find it difficult to pace myself. I need the leaves falling and the quiet blanket of winter as a reminder to stop. In the quiet, I can re-assess my internal life that lies under all the activity. In the dormancy of winter, I can find the life deep in my roots.

My daughter, Lindsey, always wanted to live in Florida, which she described as "so beautiful and tropical." Finally, she and her husband, Sergio, along with my beautiful grandson Christian moved there. Though Lindsey had always favored the tropical colors, when they returned to Illinois for an autumn visit, she appreciated the fall colors as never before. A year later, they returned like homing pigeons, once again in search of fall leaves.

My friend Marcia told me about the time she moved from the Midwest to southern California. During her first winter in the land of sunshine, she found herself so desperate for the seasonal cycle of nesting that she bought an environmental sound recording of rain, pulled all the blinds, lit all the candles, made borscht, and pretended that there was a huge storm outside.

These stories make me wonder: "Do midwesterners have an innate need for seasonal balance?" While I can't speak for all midwesterners, I do know that, just as flowers need the winter dormancy in order to bloom the following spring, all of us humans need a time of conserving our resources. Rather than the "I can do it all" mentality that can seem so enticing, necessary, and even preferable, perhaps we would do better with an "I *can't* do it all" approach, taking the time to replenish our energy when we need to. It is a great relief to concede that we are human. Frankly, I rush to that admission.

Second Wisdom: Rhythm

Because each of us is made differently, we need to discover a rhythm that supports the unique life we were created to live. Think of the creatures of the natural world. The rhythm of a bear's life, for example, follows the rhythms of the seasons in a unique way. When food is plentiful in spring and summer and early fall, bears eat like crazy, gaining up to forty pounds. During the winter months, when their food supply disappears, bears essentially sleep it off. (Sounds good!)

The seasons succeed each other in an entrancing sequence. Each of the events in the natural world is a poem, a painting, a drama, a celebration.

—Thomas Berry

Hummingbirds, on the other hand, approach the change of seasons in a completely different way. They never seem to stop moving. When I see them at my house in the summer, they are in and out at the feeders all day long, eating constantly. When it turns cold and the flowers stop blooming and the insects stop flying, there's no winter nap in sight for this active bunch. They pick up and fly a few thousand miles south to Mexico or Central America. Each creature lives its own rhythm, finding its own balance.

I picture balance as something like a juggling act. Recently, I gave a set of juggling balls to my friend Eileen's daughter, Sasha, and we all began playing with them. We quickly realized that we needed to start with one ball, and, actually, I found even that challenging. Once we felt comfortable with one ball, we added a second—which was disastrous for me. Sasha was definitely the only one with a possible future in juggling.

As I watched her, I noticed that she took time to get comfortable with each ball before she added another. I think that's one of the secrets to balanced living. First, we need to decide what is important for us, what is on our priority list. Then we need to pick up our first priority and juggle it until we feel comfortable with it before we add another. In my life and work, I have noticed that if I follow this simple guideline, I can juggle an amazing number of balls. (Not literally, of course ... I'll leave that to Sasha.)

Life doesn't require you to choose between reason and awe, or between clear-headed analysis and a rapturous sense of wonder. A balanced life includes both.

—DIANE ACKERMAN,
CULTIVATING DELIGHT

In my work as a therapist, it has taken me awhile to find a balance that works for me. I tried spreading appointments out over many days and, after many trials, eventually concentrated my appointments into three days. When I made the switch, I began to realize that when I am in "therapy mode," I am intensely present. I found that if I put in three days of therapy, I worked very hard but actually expended less energy and got more good work accomplished than if I spread it out over a full work week. My three-day work schedule left four days for recovery and enjoying other passionate pursuits—such as writing this book or spending time with the people I love. I found I could return refreshed and enlivened for another period of intensity.

I know of one person who decided things in her life had gotten so overloaded that she banned all outside activities, so she could approach this idea of balancing with a clean slate. One at a time, she added an activity back to her schedule, testing out how it felt, juggling that ball until she felt okay with it—or discarded it.

One of the things that helps me juggle the necessary pieces in my life is slowing down. I actually like doing things that shift my pace from a run to a walk. When I consciously work at *not* going faster, I am more present and aware. I'm holding off getting the faster Internet connection or the latest faster anything. I am not opposed to progress, but I definitely do not want to speed up and miss the process of my life.

My friend Pam has a beautiful art form that helps her keep inner balance. She creates lovely hand-fashioned books with

Like all who choose life in the slow lane— sailors, monks, farmers—I partake of a contemplative reality. Living close to such an expanse of land I find I have little incentive to move fast.... I have learned to trust the processes that take time.

—Kathleen Norris

159

natural handmade papers and other interesting materials, and then takes the time to write her thoughts in them. Her books are exquisite works of art and a pleasure to see and read. This feels like a very honoring and worthy process to me. We may not all want or be able to make books as Pam does, but we each need to create some space for the things that matter to us, some time apart from our daily routines.

And that, in essence, is nature's second wisdom: find the rhythm that works for you. Experiment. Juggle only what you were created to juggle. You may drop a few things in the process, but that is a great way to see what contributes to who you authentically are, and to let go of what does not work for you.

Third Wisdom: Interdependence

One of the hallmarks of North American culture is our admiration of independence, self-reliance, and individuality. We consider independence the goal of being a mature adult. For those of us baby boomers raised as part of the "me" generation, we saw independence not only as the goal, but as the epitome of success. However, what began as a celebration of individuality has too often turned into emotional isolation.

In his book *Beyond Civilization,* writer Daniel Quinn paints a bleak picture of the outcome of total self-sufficiency: "As things get worse and worse for us, we're going to need more and more of all the things that give us relief and oblivion and all the things that get us revved up and excited. More religion, more revolution, more drugs, more television channels, more sports, more casinos, more pornography, more lotteries, more access to the Web—more and more and more of it all."

Fortunately, Quinn doesn't stop there; he goes on to pose a thoughtful question: since we humans worked so well in our natural tribal culture for several million years, in a system where we each had a useful purpose contributing to the whole, why not get back to the original model? I wholeheartedly agree. Since we've veered off into competition, materialism, and independence, we've been doing pretty poorly in the quality-of-life and relationship departments.

I picture the dense matrix of the prairie. One look at its mosaic tapestry reveals its interdependency: one species seeds an area, bringing its splash of color snuggling up close to the bright flowers of a different hue, connected by grasses waving throughout. It is an interdependent system of deeply rooted plants that come together to create a strong ecosystem. Grasses make up around 60 percent of the landscape, and they literally prop up the flowering plants while enriching the soil with their deep roots. One vegetation specialist has called the prairie "the ideal prototype for community" because it is "very dynamic, interactive and cooperative.... Many species are dependent upon and contribute to other species—geology, botany, soil chemistry, wind, fire and water must all be in some sort of balance."

Neil Diboll, owner of the Prairie Nursery in Wisconsin, from which I've ordered butterfly weed forbs, describes it this way: "When you plant a community of native plants, you create a sustainable landscape and a food chain of plants and animals that coevolved for thousands of years. It's not surprising a prairie would handle a drought or attract birds."

Even though we are capable of independence, *interdependence* is a more complex and healthful way of relating. Some of us independent souls might think it easier to do things on our own,

There is a higher ecological awareness emerging, a coming into personal awareness of our interdependence with other life and our mutual responsibility.

—PRESENCE

but in the long run, it is much richer to share our experiences and loves with others.

Usually, when Leon and I moved to a new house and I was about to decorate, he would say, "Do whatever you want." I loved those words and did exactly that. As a self-directed person, it was easy for me. But when we moved from Prairie Lake and started to renovate the home we now live in, Leon suddenly had an opinion on everything. He wanted to be part of the decorating process at every bend, and I felt resistant. We negotiated paint colors, the width of the boards for the hardwood floor, the type of tile, and so on. In the end, I realized our home had a richness in look and feel that it would not have had if all the decisions had been mine. Whether I'm getting involved in "his" world, by sitting in his tree stand (as I described in chapter 4), or he is getting involved in "my" world when it comes to decorating, I am increasingly aware that Leon and I are still learning the joys of interdependence in our marriage, thirty-some years and growing.

Women are in a particularly tough spot when it comes to interdependence. We are seen as the eternal nourisher of children, of men, of society—all demanding that we give. If we're not careful, all of our time, energy, and creativeness can drain out into these channels. Anne Morrow Lindbergh touched a nerve for women in the fifties—and perhaps even more so today—with these words in her classic, *Gift from the Sea:* "Traditionally we are taught, and instinctively we long, to give

Nothing in Nature, much less conscious being, Was e'er created solely for itself.

—EDWARD YOUNG, NIGHT THOUGHTS

where it is needed—and immediately. Eternally, woman spills herself away in driblets to the thirsty, seldom being allowed the time, the quiet, the peace, to let the pitcher fill up to the brim."

In my spiritual tradition there are ultimately only two commandments. The first is to love God, and the second is to love your neighbor as yourself. The trouble is, for centuries, many well-intentioned but misguided Christians interpreted the second commandment as if it were only three words instead of five. All the emphasis was on the "love your neighbor" part, and the "as yourself" part was left to hang out in the wind. From this perspective, there is no "me," only "others."

If we think our worth is dependent on what we can give to someone else, I call that codependence. If we act as if love is *only* for someone else, we deny that we have been beautifully crafted by The Artist and are already worthy at our birth—before we have done anything. We forget the "inter" part of interdependence, the part where giving goes both ways, where love is for others *and* us. And, sadly, we forget that if we stoically pursue this one-sided giving, we may dry up and have nothing left to give. The "no me" stance is as flawed as the "only me" stance.

More and more, I am aware that "loving your neighbor" is predicated on "loving yourself." The quality and breadth and depth of the love we are able to give to others is only as much as we have learned to give to ourselves. Taking time to get our needs met creates a storehouse of energy that, in turn, allows us to reach out to others out of abundance. When we have learned

Being grounded is enhanced and renewed by periods of extended, sensuous, empathic engagement with the world, balanced by restorative moments of inward reflectiveness.

—WILLIAM CAHALAN,
ECOPSYCHOLOGY

163

to love ourselves at a core level—being intimately aware of our positive and negative characteristics, being able to care for our needs—we will have the understanding and resources to truly love another.

This is the essence of nature's third wisdom: balance giving to yourself with giving to others. Just as the grasses of the prairie take their strength from the soil's nutrients through their roots and, in turn, support their flowering neighbors, so, too, do we sometimes have energy stockpiled to share, while at other times we need to replenish our supplies. Sometimes we need help; sometimes we can give help. Sometimes we need company; sometimes we need solitude. Life is truly a balancing act, and nature gives us many opportunities to learn the beauty and gifts of interdependence.

Fourth Wisdom: The Larger Story

Many spiritual practices offer ways to rebalance our way of living and giving. I think of the motto of the Benedictine monks: *ora et labora,* "prayer and work." This balance between quiet meditation and activity in the world has been successfully guiding Benedictines for over fifteen centuries. The Jewish practice of Sabbath also comes to mind. The Sabbath is more than a twenty-four-hour break; it is a time for personal and spiritual nourishment, a time to bring the rest of the week into balance. You are probably familiar with the yin-yang symbol, which reflects the interconnectedness and balance throughout nature, a theme in Taoism. And the practices of tai chi and yoga are not only about physical balance, but also about mental, emotional, and spiritual balance. Many practitioners believe that finding a sense of physical balance is a metaphor for finding spiritual balance.

All these practices are beneficial, but there is also a universal school of balance that is available to all people, at all times: nature. Ecopsychologist Michael Cohen points out that "nature's cohesiveness has 'wired' us to relate in supportive balance." Nature is constantly replenishing and rebalancing in an inherent equilibrium. Huge varieties of plants and animals, each suited to live in a special place and in a special way, somehow come together in this amazingly balanced whole. The give-and-take laws of nature sustain life on our planet.

In this twenty-first century, we are finally coming to realize that we humans do not live on this planet alone, but in a delicate balance with all creation. When former vice president Al Gore's first book on the environment, *Earth in the Balance,* was published in 1992, many of us were hardly ready to embrace the importance of ecological balance. Yet balance was then, and should be now, both a global and personal priority. Take a moment to read what Gore wrote about balance:

> I have come to believe that the world's ecological balance depends on more than just our ability to restore a balance between civilization's ravenous appetite for resources and the fragile equilibrium of the earth's environment; it depends on more, even, than our ability to restore a balance between ourselves as individuals and the civilization we aspire to create and sustain. In the end, we must restore a balance within ourselves between who we are and what we are doing.

Are human beings fundamentally separate or inseparable from nature? We need to re-experience our place in the universe before we can see how it needs us as well as how we need it.

—PRESENCE

I think this balance "between who we are and what we are doing" is something of what it means to be a spiritual people. When we choose to weave our lives with those of others, when we cooperate with people rather than compete, when we sustain rather than deplete our world, we weave a web of connectedness that is much greater than any one of us alone. As we become more aware of, and nurtured by, the integrity, beauty, and balance in nature, we are inspired to give back. When we care for ourselves, our neighbor, and our planet, we become part of a larger story.

Therein lies the essence of nature's fourth wisdom, which I see as a circle: find your balance in the larger story, and you will find balance within yourself, and you will find balance in the larger story.... I see this circular pattern as sort of a dual consciousness, as being in both dimensions of life at once: the concrete dailyness of life and the larger life of Spirit. That is what I glimpse in Pam's journal entry, her consciousness of nature around her bringing balance to her busy day:

JANUARY—UNSEASONABLY WARM—IN THE 60S

clouds like torn flags in the wind ... a shred of blue

> *I have been running errands today ... doing things I usually put off. It seems the right thing to do ... getting aspects of my life in order that have lain neglected. Putting straight the new year.*

The deeper we look into nature, the more we recognize that it is full of life, and the more profoundly we know ... that we are united with all life that is in nature.

—ALBERT SCHWEITZER

the hawk perches on a fencepost, his wings folded

I shop for clothes—solid pieces I can layer. Ones that will keep me warm and make me happy. I finger their softness, breathing in the sweet new smell ... fabrics covering my body in colors of the season: brown, maroon, black.

dark leaves lie, decaying on the forest floor ...
resting under slate gray puddles mirroring the sky

I also buy walking shoes. Tying the laces for the first time, I set out for a walk around the lake. Soon, the soles bear witness to the journey around the path, picking up small stones and mud, leaving behind imprints matching my stride.

squirrels run along the creek bed,
their silver tails curved ... scaling barren trees

Leaving the woods, I walk along the road. Flattened, plastic bags of old newspapers litter the way. Flung off course, buried by the snows of December, their sodden weight now sinking into the earth, headlines obscured.

branches reach out, their tips forming tender buds

Focused attention produces a richness of color, a depth of sensory experience, and often means the difference between seeing and not seeing.

—LAURA SEWALL,
ECOPSYCHOLOGY

167

Fifth Wisdom and Beyond

This chapter began with the story of a cup plant. One day as I was walking a path in a Wellspring Group, I came across some of these delightful blooms. Did I tell you that this tallgrass prairie native can reach over eight feet in height? This perennial giant, sporting wonderfully cheery, yellow, daisy-like flowers, is a welcome sight during a hot midwestern summer when little else is blooming. That late summer day, I wrote in my journal:

> *Cup-plant mentor*
> *Holding water for*
> *Others*
> *Yellow flowers facing God*

Be like the flower, turn your faces to the sun.

—Kahlil Gibran

As you consider how you want to restore balance in your life, I hope you will hold the image of the cup plant—taking care of itself in drought and sharing water with birds—in your heart and mind. *The essence of nature's fifth wisdom: care for yourself and others, and always reach beyond, like the "yellow flowers facing God."*

Inspiration from a Cup Plant

- What if you slowed down and went outside to see and hear and smell and taste and touch the world around you?

- What if you noticed the sky is painted differently each day?

- What if you decided to dig in the dirt and plant some seeds?

- What if you decided to break through some concrete in your yard—or in your heart—and restore the area beneath?

- What if you saw yourself as a natural being who fit into the larger story, a bigger whole?

- What if you trusted yourself and your experience?

- What if you placed a higher value on presence to yourself and others?

- What if you started sitting on your front porch, available to the community and the neighborhood, rather than isolating yourself on the back deck?

- What if you did work that felt like it was designed for you and the end of the day was filled with satisfaction and a "good" kind of tired?

- What if you valued each of your friends and family and took the time to deeply know and enjoy them, to see with your heart, to remember their smiles and the look in their eyes?

- What if you tried another way?

- How would your life be different?

A Balancing Experience

Prepare for your journey outside with comfortable clothes that are appropriate for the weather. Take your journal and whatever art supplies, pens, and pencils you like. When you get to the place you choose, get comfy and start to relax by paying attention to your breathing and its trustworthy in and out ... in and out. Then move into this meditative exercise: When I think of balance, I think of going from one side to another and making both sides even. I think about the balance in nature and how it works with so many components. Fall moves into winter, winter into spring, spring into summer. Plants let go of seeds so there will be birth of something new. Flowers go dormant so they can bloom again. Nature gives and it also wants back. How can I reach out to others and still take time for myself?

Look around you for a symbol in nature that represents a balance of giving and receiving. Once you have found something that speaks to you, consider these questions:

- How is this a metaphor for balance in my life?

- What does this symbol teach me about following the direction of my inner compass and helping me choose my priorities?

It is never a waste of time to be outdoors, and never a waste of time to lie down and rest even for a couple of hours. It is then that images float up and then that I plan my work.

—MAY SARTON

- What can I do in my daily life to balance caring for others while still maintaining nourishment for myself?

- How can I maintain a clear, flowing wellspring while giving to others?

Reflect on your experience through meditation (just being in the moment, aware of your senses), art, journal writing, poetry, movement, photography—whatever feels right to you in the moment.

If you are undetaking this retreat with other women, gather in a circle when you come back together, and take plenty of time to share what you choose, giving each woman, in turn, your full attention. Receive what each person has to share without judgment, advice, or any attempt to fix. At this point in your journey together, I hope you are noticing that you each have your own unique way of finding what it is you need to know about your life. When everyone has finished, you might want to take time to name the things you are grateful for that have come out of this time together.

> Contemplation and prayer are like an oasis in a dry desert.... Once our reservoir is depleted, we need to return to our oasis so we don't wind up stranded in the desert without water.
>
> —JOHN MICHAEL TALBOT

Growing

As you reach the close of this book, I hope it will be the start of many more growing experiences. Take heart from the words of Kathleen Norris. In her book *Dakota: A Spiritual Geography,* she writes about living in New York and then moving to rural South Dakota where her family was rooted: "I am conscious of carrying a Plains silence within me into cities, and of carrying my city experiences back to the Plains so that they may be absorbed again back into silence, the fruitful silence that produces poems and essays."

Isn't that something of what each of us wants? To be able to move from the "city" hustle-and-bustle of our everyday lives, into the silence of nature and our inner spirit, and back again? To experience the "fruitful silence" that produces creative expression? To be fully ourselves, spiritually restored, with our wellspring clear and flowing?

Spiritual people have the ability to dream beyond what they know. They are hopeful, alive, and intuitive. They operate out of a model of generosity and love because they know there is plenty. The more they give away, the more they get to give away. There is an ease and humor in truly spiritual people. I think part of this freedom and joy comes from knowing the world doesn't rest on their shoulders and a belief in something greater than themselves.

As you walk your prairie—or your city park or backyard or a local nature preserve—I hope you will awaken to your depths as a spiritual person, fully connected with your authentic self through the exploration of nature and the nurture of Spirit. May you truly experience the mystery, grace, and beauty of your full self as part of The Creator's artwork on our beautiful planet Earth.

Be who you are and say what you feel because those who mind don't matter and those who matter don't mind.

—Dr. Seuss

Welcoming

Thirty-seven minutes after writing the last word of this book, Leon and I walked through fresh white snow into the local hospital to welcome our dear new grandson, Cameron John Chickerneo, a lovely creation fresh from The Artist, born to Jay and Amy thirty minutes earlier at 11:07 p.m. This sweet baby reminded me that all things are always new in this beautiful creation we share. I am thankful. I want to remain fully alive and present to the moments.

I hope you have enjoyed and been enlivened by reading and experiencing *Woman Spirit Awakening in Nature,* whether it has been a solitary journey or one in community with others. I invite you to check out www.spasisters.org and join us in the SPA Sisters Program for fun and a deeper experience of your life. I have participated in countless Awakening Retreats and Wellspring Groups, and there is new learning for me every time. You are always welcome.

All my life through, the new sights of Nature made me rejoice like a child.

—MARIE CURIE

The program consists of a one-day Awakening Retreat followed by an optional six-week Wellspring Group. Each gathering includes an experience of solitude in nature, with time for recording your experience in a journal with poetry, writing, and drawings, and then sharing in community and discussion with other women. During the time alone in nature, there is an emphasis on being aware of your senses and of what you are attracted to in nature. The Awakening Retreat opens you to an experience of your beauty and value, and encourages reflection through the use of creative tools. The Wellspring Group takes you on an exploration to discover what you need to restore your clear, free-flowing spirit. Starting with a re-introduction to your child energy in nature via early recollections, the process moves through letting go of what is holding you back, nurturing new priorities, and rebalancing your life so you can grow into the fullness of who you are.

SPA Sisters is a nonprofit educational program. If you are interested in attending a SPA Sisters event, we'd be glad to hear from you. We are even happy to set up one for you and your friends at a time and place that works for you. We have scholarships for those who need it and are delighted with tax-deductible gifts for those who want to "pay it forward." If you are a professional in the mental health field and are interested in SPA Sisters therapist training, contact us about coming to an event. Check out our website at www.spasisters.org for more information.

Thanking

I am grateful to you, Patty Martindale, Sandy Alcorn, Susan Schor, Anne Utterback, Gail Castle, Marie Egeland, Pam Allnutt, Deb Marqui, and Eileen Fisher for sharing the beauty and truth in your lives through your stories and encouragement with the writing of this book. And thanks also to Eileen for writing the wonderful foreword and to Shanti Durkee for the sweet cover design. Thanks to John Lionberger for pointing me to the good people of SkyLight Paths Publishing and especially to Emily Wichland, vice president of Editorial and Production, who recognized the value of this book and connected me with Marcia Broucek, who is an editor extraordinaire, both brilliant and creative! Thank you to my daughter, Lindsey De Los Santos, for helping create the SPA Sisters Program that seeded this book. Gratitude to Cheryl Campbell, Jan Torrance, Merikay Huszagh, Marg Rehnberg, A. J. Madonia, Therese Yonikus, Cindy Johnson, Nina Madonia, Patti Chickerneo, and Nancy Andrews for feedback and encouragement. Also thanks to my son, Jay Chickerneo, who created the spasisters.org website and consistently prayed with his wife, Amy, about this work, as did Gary McCormick, Lynn Zuk-Loyd, my husband, Leon, and many of the others above. I am always thankful to Leon for being an undergirding force in our family where creative energy grows and flourishes!

Reading

Anderson, Lorraine, ed. *Sisters of the Earth: Women's Prose and Poetry about Nature*. New York: Vintage Books, 2003.

Armstrong, Jeanette. "Keepers of the Earth." In *Ecopsychology: Restoring the Earth, Healing the Mind,* edited by Theodore Roszak, Mary E. Gomes, and Allen D. Kanner, 316–324. San Francisco: Sierra Club Books, 1995.

Berry, Thomas. *The Great Work: Our Way into the Future.* New York: Bell Tower, 1999.

Berry, Wendell. *The Art of the Commonplace.* Washington, DC: Shoemaker and Hoard, 2002.

Chard, Philip Sutton. *The Healing Earth: Nature's Medicine for the Troubled Soul.* Minocqua, WI: Northword Press, Inc., 1994.

Chilson, Richard. *All Will Be Well: Based on the Classic Spirituality of Julian of Norwich.* Notre Dame, IN: Ave Maria Press, 2003.

Cohen, Michael J. *Reconnecting with Nature: Finding Wellness through Restoring Your Bond with the Earth.* Corvallis, OR: Ecopress, 1997.

D'Arcy, Paula. *Gift of the Red Bird: A Spiritual Encounter.* New York: The Crossroad Publishing Company, 1996.

Deignan, Kathleen, ed. *When the Trees Say Nothing: Writings on Nature by Thomas Merton.* Notre Dame, IN: Sorin Books, 2003.

Dillard, Annie. *Pilgrim at Tinker Creek*. New York: Harper Collins Publishers, 1998.

Estes, Clarissa Pinkola. *Women Who Run with the Wolves: Myths and Stories of the Wild Woman Archetype*. New York: Ballantine Books, 1992.

Fox, Matthew. *Breakthrough: Meister Eckhart's Creation Spirituality in New Translation*. Garden City, NY: Doubleday & Company, 1980.

——. *Illuminations of Hildegard of Bingen*. Santa Fe, NM: Bear and Company, 1985.

Franck, Frederick. *The Zen of Seeing: Seeing/Drawing as Meditation*. New York: Vintage Books, 1973.

Gardner, Howard. *Frames of Mind: The Theory of Multiple Intelligences*. New York: Basic Books, 1983/2003.

Glendinning, Chellis. *My Name Is Chellis and I'm in Recovery from Western Civilization*. Boston, MA: Shambhala Publications, 1994.

Gore, Al. *Earth in the Balance: Ecology and the Human Spirit*. Emmaus, PA: Rodale, 2006.

——. *An Inconvenient Truth: The Planetary Emergency of Global Warming and What We Can Do about It*. Emmaus, PA: Rodale, 2006.

Hurd, Barbara. *Stirring the Mud: On Swamps, Bogs, and Human Imagination*. New York: Houghton Mifflin, 2003.

Lauber, Patricia. *Painters of the Caves*. Washington, DC: National Geographic Society, 1998.

Leopold, Aldo. *A Sand County Almanac and Sketches Here and There*. Oxford: Oxford University Press, 1949.

Lindbergh, Anne Morrow. *Gift from the Sea*. New York: Random House, 1991.

Lionberger, John. *Renewal in the Wilderness: A Spiritual Guide to Connecting with God in the Natural World*. Woodstock, VT: SkyLight Paths Publishing, 2007.

London, Peter. *Drawing Closer to Nature: Making Art in Dialogue with the Natural World*. Boston: Shambhala Publications, 2003.

Louv, Richard. *Last Child in the Woods: Saving Our Children from Nature-Deficit Disorder.* New York: Algonquin Books of Chapel Hill, 2005.

Madson, John. *Where the Sky Began: Land of the Tallgrass Prairie.* Boston: Houghton Mifflin, 1982.

Merton, Thomas. *Thoughts in Solitude.* New York: Farrar, Straus and Giroux, 1999.

———. *When the Trees Say Nothing: Writings on Nature.* Notre Dame, IN: Sorin Books, 2003.

Muir, John. *My First Summer in the Sierra.* Boston: Houghton Mifflin, 1911.

Norris, Kathleen. *Dakota: A Spiritual Geography.* New York: Houghton Mifflin, 1993.

Quinn, Daniel. *Beyond Civilization: Humanity's Next Great Adventure.* New York: Three Rivers Press, 1999.

Remen, Rachel Naomi. *Kitchen Table Wisdom: Stories That Heal.* New York: Riverhead Books, 1996.

Roszak, Theodore. *The Voice of the Earth: An Exploration of Ecopsychology.* New York: Simon & Schuster, 1992.

Roszak, Theodore, Mary E. Gomes, and Allen D. Kanner, eds. *Ecopsychology: Restoring the Earth, Healing the Mind.* San Francisco: Sierra Book Club, 1995.

Sabini, Meredith, ed. *The Earth Has a Soul: The Nature Writings by C. G. Jung.* Berkeley, CA: North Atlantic Books, 2002.

Sarton, May. *Journal of a Solitude.* New York: W. W. Norton, 1973.

Scott, Susan S. *Healing with Nature.* New York: Helios Press, 2003.

Senge, Peter, C., Otto Scharmer, Joseph Jaworski, and Betty Sue Flowers. *Presence: Human Purpose and the Field of the Future.* Cambridge, MA: The Society for Organizational Learning, 2004.

Swimme, Brian. *Canticle to the Cosmos.* DVD. San Francisco: Tides Center, 1990.

Talbot, John Michael. *The Lessons of St. Francis: How to Bring Simplicity and Spirituality into Your Daily Life.* New York: Penguin Putnam, 1998.

Teilhard de Chardin, Pierre. "Forma Christ" (1918). In *Writings in Time of War.* New York: Harper & Row, 1968.

Thoreau, Henry David. *Letters to a Spiritual Seeker.* New York: W. W. Norton, 2004.

——. *Walden.* Boston: Houghton Mifflin, 2004.

Credits

About the Author

Nancy Barrett Chickerneo, PhD, is director of SPA Sisters: Spirit, Place and Authentic Self®, a non-profit organization whose mission is to inspire, educate, and awaken women to their true selves through interaction with nature, creative  expression, and connection with other women. A licensed clinical professional counselor and registered art therapist, Nancy is also a professional watercolor artist. One of her greatest passions is helping women come to wholeness and she enjoys joining creativity and spirituality in the workshops and retreats she leads.

Eileen Fisher is a well-known designer of women's clothing, and Chief Creative Officer of Eileen Fisher, Inc., which is committed to supporting women in many ways.

Journaling

Journaling

Journaling

Journaling

Journaling

Journaling

Journaling

Journaling

Journaling

Journaling

Journaling

Journaling

Journaling

Journaling

Journaling

Journaling

Children's Spirituality

Remembering My Grandparent: A Kid's Own Grief Workbook in the Christian Tradition
by Nechama Liss-Levinson, PhD, and Rev. Molly Phinney Baskette, MDiv
8 x 10, 48 pp, 2-color text, HC, 978-1-59473-212-6 **$16.99** *For ages 7–13*

Does God Ever Sleep? *by Joan Sauro, CSJ; Full-color photos*
A charming nighttime reminder that God is always present in our lives.
10 x 8½, 32 pp, Quality PB, Full-color photos, 978-1-59473-110-5 **$8.99** *For ages 3–6*

Does God Forgive Me? *by August Gold; Full-color photos by Diane Hardy Waller*
Gently shows how God forgives all that we do if we are truly sorry.
10 x 8½, 32 pp, Quality PB, Full-color photos, 978-1-59473-142-6 **$8.99** *For ages 3–6*

God Said Amen *by Sandy Eisenberg Sasso; Full-color illus. by Avi Katz*
A warm and inspiring tale of two kingdoms that shows us that we need only reach out to each other to find the answers to our prayers.
9 x 12, 32 pp, HC, Full-color illus., 978-1-58023-080-3 **$16.95** *For ages 4 & up (a Jewish Lights book)*

How Does God Listen? *by Kay Lindahl; Full-color photos by Cynthia Maloney*
How do we know when God is listening to us? Children will find the answers to these questions as they engage their senses while the story unfolds, learning how God listens in the wind, waves, clouds, hot chocolate, perfume, our tears and our laughter.
10 x 8½, 32 pp, Quality PB, Full-color photos, 978-1-59473-084-9 **$8.99** *For ages 3–6*

In God's Hands *by Lawrence Kushner and Gary Schmidt; Full-color illus. by Matthew J. Baeck*
9 x 12, 32 pp, Full-color illus., HC, 978-1-58023-224-1 **$16.99** *For ages 5 & up (a Jewish Lights book)*

In God's Name *by Sandy Eisenberg Sasso; Full-color illus. by Phoebe Stone*
Like an ancient myth in its poetic text and vibrant illustrations, this award-winning modern fable about the search for God's name celebrates the diversity and, at the same time, the unity of all the people of the world.
9 x 12, 32 pp, HC, Full-color illus., 978-1-879045-26-2 **$16.99** *For ages 4 & up (a Jewish Lights book)*

Also available in Spanish: El nombre de Dios
9 x 12, 32 pp, HC, Full-color illus., 978-1-893361-63-8 **$16.95**

In Our Image: God's First Creatures *by Nancy Sohn Swartz; Full-color illus. by Melanie Hall*
A playful new twist on the Genesis story—from the perspective of the animals. Celebrates the interconnectedness of nature and the harmony of all living things.
9 x 12, 32 pp, HC, Full-color illus., 978-1-879045-99-6 **$16.95** *For ages 4 & up (a Jewish Lights book)*

Noah's Wife: The Story of Naamah
by Sandy Eisenberg Sasso; Full-color illus. by Bethanne Andersen
This new story, based on an ancient text, opens readers' religious imaginations to new ideas about the well-known story of the Flood. When God tells Noah to bring the animals of the world onto the ark, God also calls on Naamah, Noah's wife, to save each plant on Earth.
9 x 12, 32 pp, HC, Full-color illus., 978-1-58023-134-3 **$16.95** *For ages 4 & up (a Jewish Lights book)*

Also available: Naamah: Noah's Wife (A Board Book)
by Sandy Eisenberg Sasso; Full-color illus. by Bethanne Andersen
5 x 5, 24 pp, Board Book, Full-color illus., 978-1-893361-56-0 **$7.99** *For ages 0–4*

Where Does God Live? *by August Gold and Matthew J. Perlman*
Using simple, everyday examples that children can relate to, this colorful book helps young readers develop a personal understanding of God.
10 x 8½, 32 pp, Quality PB, Full-color photo illus., 978-1-893361-39-3 **$8.99** *For ages 3–6*

Children's Spirituality—Board Books

Adam and Eve's New Day (A Board Book)
by Sandy Eisenberg Sasso; Full-color illus. by Joani Keller Rothenberg
A lesson in hope for every child who has worried about what comes next. Abridged from *Adam and Eve's First Sunset*. 5 x 5, 24 pp, Full-color illus., Board Book, 978-1-59473-205-8 **$7.99** *For ages 0–4*

How Did the Animals Help God? (A Board Book)
by Nancy Sohn Swartz; Full-color illus. by Melanie Hall
Abridged from *In Our Image*, God asks all of nature to offer gifts to humankind—with a promise that they will care for creation in return.
5 x 5, 24 pp, Board Book, Full-color illus., 978-1-59473-044-3 **$7.99** *For ages 0–4*

Where Is God? (A Board Book) *by Lawrence and Karen Kushner; Full-color illus. by*
Dawn W. Majewski A gentle way for young children to explore how God is with us every day, in every way. Abridged from *Because Nothing Looks Like God*.
5 x 5, 24 pp, Board Book, Full-color illus., 978-1-893361-17-1 **$7.99** *For ages 0–4*

What Does God Look Like? (A Board Book)
by Lawrence and Karen Kushner; Full-color illus. by Dawn W. Majewski
A simple way for young children to explore the ways that we "see" God. Abridged from *Because Nothing Looks Like God*. 5 x 5, 24 pp, Board Book, Full-color illus., 978-1-893361-23-2 **$7.99** *For ages 0–4*

How Does God Make Things Happen? (A Board Book)
by Lawrence and Karen Kushner; Full-color illus. by Dawn W. Majewski
A charming invitation for young children to explore how God makes things happen in our world. Abridged from *Because Nothing Looks Like God*.
5 x 5, 24 pp, Board Book, Full-color illus., 978-1-893361-24-9 **$7.99** *For ages 0–4*

What Is God's Name? (A Board Book)
by Sandy Eisenberg Sasso; Full-color illus. by Phoebe Stone
Everyone and everything in the world has a name. What is God's name? Abridged from the award-winning *In God's Name*. 5 x 5, 24 pp, Board Book, Full-color illus., 978-1-893361-10-2 **$7.99** *For ages 0–4*

What You Will See Inside ...

This important new series of books, each with many full-color photos, is designed to show children ages 6 and up the Who, What, When, Where, Why and How of traditional houses of worship, liturgical celebrations, and rituals of different world faiths, empowering them to respect and understand their own religious traditions—and those of their friends and neighbors.

What You Will See Inside a Catholic Church
by Reverend Michael Keane; Foreword by Robert J. Keeley, EdD; Full-color photos by Aaron Pepis
8½ x 10½, 32 pp, Full-color photos, HC, 978-1-893361-54-6 **$17.95**
Also available in Spanish: **Lo que se puede ver dentro de una iglesia católica**
8½ x 10½, 32 pp, Full-color photos, HC, 978-1-893361-66-9 **$16.95**

What You Will See Inside a Hindu Temple
by Dr. Mahendra Jani and Dr. Vandana Jani; Full-color photos by Neirah Bhargava and Vijay Dave
8½ x 10½, 32 pp, Full-color photos, HC, 978-1-59473-116-7 **$17.99**

What You Will See Inside a Mosque *by Aisha Karen Khan; Full-color photos by Aaron Pepis*
8½ x 10½, 32 pp, Full-color photos, HC, 978-1-893361-60-7 **$16.95**

What You Will See Inside a Synagogue
by Rabbi Lawrence A. Hoffman and Dr. Ron Wolfson; Full-color photos by Bill Aron
8½ x 10½, 32 pp, Full-color photos, HC, 978-1-59473-012-2 **$17.99**

Children's Spiritual Biography

Ten Amazing People
And How They Changed the World
by Maura D. Shaw; Foreword by Dr. Robert Coles
Full-color illus. by Stephen Marchesi

For ages 7 & up

Black Elk • Dorothy Day • Malcolm X • Mahatma Gandhi • Martin Luther King, Jr. • Mother Teresa • Janusz Korczak • Desmond Tutu • Thich Nhat Hanh • Albert Schweitzer

This vivid, inspirational and authoritative book will open new possibilities for children by telling the stories of how ten of the past century's greatest leaders changed the world in important ways.

8½ x 11, 48 pp, HC, Full-color illus., 978-1-893361-47-8 **$17.95** *For ages 7 & up*

Spiritual Biographies for Young People—For ages 7 and up

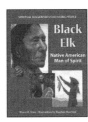 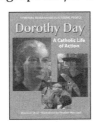 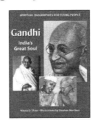 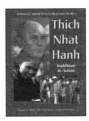

Black Elk: Native American Man of Spirit *by Maura D. Shaw; Full-color illus. by Stephen Marchesi*
Through historically accurate illustrations and photos, inspiring age-appropriate activities and Black Elk's own words, this colorful biography introduces children to a remarkable person who ensured that the traditions and beliefs of his people would not be forgotten.
6¾ x 8¾, 32 pp, HC, Full-color and b/w illus., 978-1-59473-043-6 **$12.99**

Dorothy Day: A Catholic Life of Action *by Maura D. Shaw; Full-color illus. by Stephen Marchesi*
Introduces children to one of the most inspiring women of the twentieth century, a down-to-earth spiritual leader who saw the presence of God in every person she met. Includes practical activities, a timeline and a list of important words to know.
6¾ x 8¾, 32 pp, HC, Full-color illus., 978-1-59473-011-5 **$12.99**

Gandhi: India's Great Soul *by Maura D. Shaw; Full-color illus. by Stephen Marchesi*
There are a number of biographies of Gandhi written for young readers, but this is the only one that balances a simple text with illustrations, photographs, and activities that encourage children and adults to talk about how to make changes happen without violence. Introduces children to important concepts of freedom, equality and justice among people of all backgrounds and religions.
6¾ x 8¾, 32 pp, HC, Full-color illus., 978-1-893361-91-1 **$12.95**

Thich Nhat Hanh: Buddhism in Action *by Maura D. Shaw; Full-color illus. by Stephen Marchesi*
Warm illustrations, photos, age-appropriate activities and Thich Nhat Hanh's own poems introduce a great man to children in a way they can understand and enjoy. Includes a list of important Buddhist words to know.
6¾ x 8¾, 32 pp, HC, Full-color illus., 978-1-893361-87-4 **$12.95**

Midrash Fiction / Folktales

Abraham's Bind & Other Bible Tales of Trickery, Folly, Mercy and Love
by Michael J. Caduto
New retellings of episodes in the lives of familiar biblical characters explore relevant life lessons.
6 x 9, 224 pp, HC, 978-1-59473-186-0 **$19.99**

Daughters of the Desert: Stories of Remarkable Women from Christian, Jewish and Muslim
Traditions   *by Claire Rudolf Murphy, Meghan Nuttall Sayres, Mary Cronk Farrell, Sarah Conover and Betsy Wharton*
Breathes new life into the old tales of our female ancestors in faith. Uses traditional scriptural passages as starting points, then with vivid detail fills in historical context and place. Chapters reveal the voices of Sarah, Hagar, Huldah, Esther, Salome, Mary Magdalene, Lydia, Khadija, Fatima and many more. Historical fiction ideal for readers of all ages. Quality paperback includes reader's discussion guide.
5½ x 8½, 192 pp, Quality PB, 978-1-59473-106-8 **$14.99** HC, 192 pp, 978-1-893361-72-0 **$19.95**

The Triumph of Eve & Other Subversive Bible Tales
by Matt Biers-Ariel
Many people were taught and remember only a one-dimensional Bible. These engaging retellings are the antidote to this—they're witty, often hilarious, always profound, and invite you to grapple with questions and issues that are often hidden in the original text.
5½ x 8½, 192 pp, Quality PB, 978-1-59473-176-1 **$14.99**
Also avail.: **The Triumph of Eve Teacher's Guide**
8½ x 11, 44 pp, PB, 978-1-59473-152-5 **$8.99**

Wisdom in the Telling
Finding Inspiration and Grace in Traditional Folktales and Myths Retold
by Lorraine Hartin-Gelardi 6 x 9, 224 pp, HC, 978-1-59473-185-3 **$19.99**

Religious Etiquette / Reference

How to Be a Perfect Stranger, 4th Edition: The Essential Religious Etiquette Handbook
Edited by Stuart M. Matlins and Arthur J. Magida
The indispensable guidebook to help the well-meaning guest when visiting other people's religious ceremonies. A straightforward guide to the rituals and celebrations of the major religions and denominations in the United States and Canada from the perspective of an interested guest of any other faith, based on information obtained from authorities of each religion. Belongs in every living room, library and office. Covers:
African American Methodist Churches • Assemblies of God • Bahá'í • Baptist • Buddhist • Christian Church (Disciples of Christ) • Christian Science (Church of Christ, Scientist) • Churches of Christ • Episcopalian and Anglican • Hindu • Islam • Jehovah's Witnesses • Jewish • Lutheran • Mennonite/Amish • Methodist • Mormon (Church of Jesus Christ of Latter-day Saints) • Native American/First Nations • Orthodox Churches • Pentecostal Church of God • Presbyterian • Quaker (Religious Society of Friends) • Reformed Church in America/Canada • Roman Catholic • Seventh-day Adventist • Sikh • Unitarian Universalist • United Church of Canada • United Church of Christ
6 x 9, 432 pp, Quality PB, 978-1-59473-140-2 **$19.99**

The Perfect Stranger's Guide to Funerals and Grieving Practices: A Guide to Etiquette in Other
People's Religious Ceremonies   *Edited by Stuart M. Matlins*
6 x 9, 240 pp, Quality PB, 978-1-893361-20-1 **$16.95**

The Perfect Stranger's Guide to Wedding Ceremonies: A Guide to Etiquette in Other People's
Religious Ceremonies   *Edited by Stuart M. Matlins*
6 x 9, 208 pp, Quality PB, 978-1-893361-19-5 **$16.95**

Spiritual Biography / Reference

Spiritual Leaders Who Changed the World
The Essential Handbook to the Past Century of Religion
Edited by Ira Rifkin and the Editors at SkyLight Paths; Foreword by Dr. Robert Coles
An invaluable reference to the most important spiritual leaders of the past 100 years.
6 x 9, 304 pp, 15+ b/w photos, Quality PB, 978-1-59473-241-6 **$18.99**

Spiritual Biography—SkyLight Lives

SkyLight Lives reintroduces the lives and works of key spiritual figures of our time—people who by their teaching or example have challenged our assumptions about spirituality and have caused us to look at it in new ways.

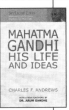

The Life of Evelyn Underhill
An Intimate Portrait of the Groundbreaking Author of Mysticism
by Margaret Cropper; Foreword by Dana Greene
Evelyn Underhill was a passionate writer and teacher who wrote elegantly on mysticism, worship, and devotional life.
6 x 9, 288 pp, 5 b/w photos, Quality PB, 978-1-893361-70-6 **$18.95**

Mahatma Gandhi: His Life and Ideas
by Charles F. Andrews; Foreword by Dr. Arun Gandhi
Examines from a contemporary Christian activist's point of view the religious ideas and political dynamics that influenced the birth of the peaceful resistance movement.
6 x 9, 336 pp, 5 b/w photos, Quality PB, 978-1-893361-89-8 **$18.95**

Simone Weil: A Modern Pilgrimage *by Robert Coles*
The extraordinary life of the spiritual philosopher who's been called both saint and madwoman.
6 x 9, 208 pp, Quality PB, 978-1-893361-34-8 **$16.95**

Zen Effects: The Life of Alan Watts
by Monica Furlong
Through his widely popular books and lectures, Alan Watts (1915–1973) did more to introduce Eastern philosophy and religion to Western minds than any figure before or since.
6 x 9, 264 pp, Quality PB, 978-1-893361-32-4 **$16.95**

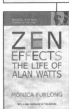

More Spiritual Biography

Bede Griffiths: An Introduction to His Interspiritual Thought
by Wayne Teasdale
The first study of his contemplative experience and thought, exploring the intersection of Hinduism and Christianity.
6 x 9, 288 pp, Quality PB, 978-1-893361-77-5 **$18.95**

The Soul of the Story: Meetings with Remarkable People
by Rabbi David Zeller
Inspiring and entertaining, this compelling collection of spiritual adventures assures us that no spiritual lesson truly learned is ever lost.
6 x 9, 288 pp, HC, 978-1-58023-272-2 **$21.99** *(a Jewish Lights book)*

Prayer / Meditation

Sacred Attention: A Spiritual Practice for Finding God in the Moment *by Margaret D. McGee*
Framed on the Christian liturgical year, this inspiring guide explores ways to develop a practice of attention as a means of talking—and listening—to God. 6 x 9, 144 pp, HC, 978-1-59473-232-4 **$19.99**

Women Pray: Voices through the Ages, from Many Faiths, Cultures and Traditions
Edited and with Introductions by Monica Furlong 5 x 7¼, 256 pp, Quality PB, 978-1-59473-071-9 **$15.99**

Women of Color Pray: Voices of Strength, Faith, Healing,
Hope and Courage *Edited and with Introductions by Christal M. Jackson*
Through these prayers, poetry, lyrics, meditations and affirmations, you will share in the strong and undeniable connection women of color share with God. 5 x 7¼, 208 pp, Quality PB, 978-1-59473-077-1 **$15.99**

Secrets of Prayer: A Multifaith Guide to Creating Personal Prayer in Your Life
by Nancy Corcoran, CSJ
This compelling, multifaith guidebook offers you companionship and encouragement on the journey to a healthy prayer life. 6 x 9, 160 pp, Quality PB, 978-1-59473-215-7 **$16.99**

Prayers to an Evolutionary God   *by William Cleary; Afterword by Diarmuid O'Murchu*
Inspired by the spiritual and scientific teachings of Diarmuid O'Murchu and Teilhard de Chardin, reveals that religion and science can be combined to create an expanding view of the universe—an evolutionary faith. 6 x 9, 208 pp, HC, 978-1-59473-006-1 **$21.99**

The Art of Public Prayer: Not for Clergy Only   *by Lawrence A. Hoffman*
6 x 9, 288 pp, Quality PB, 978-1-893361-06-5 **$18.99**

A Heart of Stillness: A Complete Guide to Learning the Art of Meditation
by David A. Cooper 5½ x 8½, 272 pp, Quality PB, 978-1-893361-03-4 **$16.95**

Meditation without Gurus: A Guide to the Heart of Practice
by Clark Strand 5½ x 8½, 192 pp, Quality PB, 978-1-893361-93-5 **$16.95**

Praying with Our Hands: 21 Practices of Embodied Prayer from the World's Spiritual Traditions
by Jon M. Sweeney; Photographs by Jennifer J. Wilson; Foreword by Mother Tessa Bielecki; Afterword by Taitetsu Unno, PhD
8 x 8, 96 pp, 22 duotone photos, Quality PB, 978-1-893361-16-4 **$16.95**

Silence, Simplicity & Solitude: A Complete Guide to Spiritual Retreat at Home
by David A. Cooper 5½ x 8½, 336 pp, Quality PB, 978-1-893361-04-1 **$16.95**

Three Gates to Meditation Practice: A Personal Journey into Sufism, Buddhism, and Judaism
by David A. Cooper 5½ x 8½, 240 pp, Quality PB, 978-1-893361-22-5 **$16.95**

Prayer / M. Basil Pennington, OCSO

Finding Grace at the Center, 3rd Ed.: The Beginning of Centering Prayer
with Thomas Keating, OCSO, and Thomas E. Clarke, SJ; Foreword by Rev. Cynthia Bourgeault, PhD
A practical guide to a simple and beautiful form of meditative prayer.
5 x 7¼, 128 pp, Quality PB, 978-1-59473-182-2 **$12.99**

The Monks of Mount Athos: A Western Monk's Extraordinary Spiritual Journey on Eastern
Holy Ground   *Foreword by Archimandrite Dionysios*
Explores the landscape, the monastic communities, and the food of Athos.
6 x 9, 256 pp, 10+ b/w drawings, Quality PB, 978-1-893361-78-2 **$18.95**

Psalms: A Spiritual Commentary   *Illustrations by Phillip Ratner*
Reflections on some of the most beloved passages from the Bible's most widely read book.
6 x 9, 176 pp, 24 full-page b/w illus., Quality PB, 978-1-59473-234-8 **$16.99** HC, 978-1-59473-141-9 **$19.99**

The Song of Songs: A Spiritual Commentary   *Illustrations by Phillip Ratner*
Explore the Bible's most challenging mystical text.
6 x 9, 160 pp, 14 b/w illus., Quality PB, 978-1-59473-235-3 **$16.99**; HC, 978-1-59473-004-7 **$19.99**

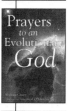

Spiritual Poetry—The Mystic Poets

Experience these mystic poets as you never have before. Each beautiful, compact book includes: a brief introduction to the poet's time and place; a summary of the major themes of the poet's mysticism and religious tradition; essential selections from the poet's most important works; and an appreciative preface by a contemporary spiritual writer.

Hafiz
The Mystic Poets
Preface by Ibrahim Gamard
Hafiz is known throughout the world as Persia's greatest poet, with sales of his poems in Iran today only surpassed by those of the Qur'an itself. His probing and joyful verse speaks to people from all backgrounds who long to taste and feel divine love and experience harmony with all living things.
5 x 7¼, 144 pp, HC, 978-1-59473-009-2 **$16.99**

Hopkins
The Mystic Poets
Preface by Rev. Thomas Ryan, CSP
Gerard Manley Hopkins, Christian mystical poet, is beloved for his use of fresh language and startling metaphors to describe the world around him. Although his verse is lovely, beneath the surface lies a searching soul, wrestling with and yearning for God.
5 x 7¼, 112 pp, HC, 978-1-59473-010-8 **$16.99**

Tagore
The Mystic Poets
Preface by Swami Adiswarananda
Rabindranath Tagore is often considered the "Shakespeare" of modern India. A great mystic, Tagore was the teacher of W. B. Yeats and Robert Frost, the close friend of Albert Einstein and Mahatma Gandhi, and the winner of the Nobel Prize for Literature. This beautiful sampling of Tagore's two most important works, *The Gardener* and *Gitanjali*, offers a glimpse into his spiritual vision that has inspired people around the world.
5 x 7¼, 144 pp, HC, 978-1-59473-008-5 **$16.99**

Whitman
The Mystic Poets
Preface by Gary David Comstock
Walt Whitman was the most innovative and influential poet of the nineteenth century. This beautiful sampling of Whitman's most important poetry from *Leaves of Grass,* and selections from his prose writings, offers a glimpse into the spiritual side of his most radical themes—love for country, love for others, and love of Self.
5 x 7¼, 192 pp, HC, 978-1-59473-041-2 **$16.99**

Journeys of Simplicity
Traveling Light with Thomas Merton, Bashō,
Edward Abbey, Annie Dillard & Others
Invites you to consider a more graceful way of traveling through life. Use the included journal pages (in PB only) to help you get started on your own spiritual journey.

by Philip Harnden
5 x 7¼, 144 pp, Quality PB, 978-1-59473-181-5 **$12.99**   128 pp, HC, 978-1-893361-76-8 **$16.95**

Spirituality of the Seasons

Autumn: A Spiritual Biography of the Season
Edited by Gary Schmidt and Susan M. Felch; Illustrations by Mary Azarian
Rejoice in autumn as a time of preparation and reflection. Includes Wendell Berry, David James Duncan, Robert Frost, A. Bartlett Giamatti, E. B. White, P. D. James, Julian of Norwich, Garret Keizer, Tracy Kidder, Anne Lamott, May Sarton. 6 x 9, 320 pp, 5 b/w illus., Quality PB, 978-1-59473-118-1 **$18.99**

Spring: A Spiritual Biography of the Season
Edited by Gary Schmidt and Susan M. Felch; Illustrations by Mary Azarian
Explore the gentle unfurling of spring and reflect on how nature celebrates rebirth and renewal. Includes Jane Kenyon, Lucy Larcom, Harry Thurston, Nathaniel Hawthorne, Noel Perrin, Annie Dillard, Martha Ballard, Barbara Kingsolver, Dorothy Wordsworth, Donald Hall, David Brill, Lionel Basney, Isak Dinesen, Paul Laurence Dunbar. 6 x 9, 352 pp, 6 b/w illus., Quality PB, 978-1-59473-246-1 **$18.99**

Summer: A Spiritual Biography of the Season
Edited by Gary Schmidt and Susan M. Felch; Illustrations by Barry Moser
"A sumptuous banquet.... These selections lift up an exquisite wholeness found within an everyday sophistication."— ★ *Publishers Weekly* starred review
Includes Anne Lamott, Luci Shaw, Ray Bradbury, Richard Selzer, Thomas Lynch, Walt Whitman, Carl Sandburg, Sherman Alexie, Madeleine L'Engle, Jamaica Kincaid.
6 x 9, 304 pp, 5 b/w illus., 978-1-59473-183-9 **$18.99** HC, 978-1-59473-083-2 **$21.99**

Winter: A Spiritual Biography of the Season
Edited by Gary Schmidt and Susan M. Felch; Illustrations by Barry Moser
"This outstanding anthology features top-flight nature and spirituality writers on the fierce, inexorable season of winter.... Remarkably lively and warm, despite the icy subject." — ★ *Publishers Weekly* starred review
Includes Will Campbell, Rachel Carson, Annie Dillard, Donald Hall, Ron Hansen, Jane Kenyon, Jamaica Kincaid, Barry Lopez, Kathleen Norris, John Updike, E. B. White.
6 x 9, 288 pp, 6 b/w illus., Deluxe PB w/flaps, 978-1-893361-92-8 **$18.95** HC, 978-1-893361-53-9 **$21.95**

Spirituality / Animal Companions

Blessing the Animals: Prayers and Ceremonies to Celebrate God's Creatures, Wild and Tame
Edited by Lynn L. Caruso 5 x 7¼, 256 pp, HC, 978-1-59473-145-7 **$19.99**

Remembering My Pet: A Kid's Own Spiritual Workbook for When a Pet Dies
by Nechama Liss-Levinson, PhD, and Rev. Molly Phinney Baskette, MDiv; Foreword by Lynn L. Caruso
8 x 10, 48 pp, 2-color text, HC, 978-1-59473-221-3 **$16.99**

What Animals Can Teach Us about Spirituality: Inspiring Lessons from Wild and Tame Creatures
by Diana L. Guerrero 6 x 9, 176 pp, Quality PB, 978-1-893361-84-3 **$16.95**

Spirituality—A Week Inside

Come and Sit: A Week Inside Meditation Centers *by Marcia Z. Nelson; Foreword by Wayne Teasdale*
6 x 9, 224 pp, b/w photos, Quality PB, 978-1-893361-35-5 **$16.95**

Lighting the Lamp of Wisdom: A Week Inside a Yoga Ashram *by John Ittner; Foreword by Dr. David Frawley*
6 x 9, 192 pp, 10+ b/w photos, Quality PB, 978-1-893361-52-2 **$15.95**

Making a Heart for God: A Week Inside a Catholic Monastery
by Dianne Aprile; Foreword by Brother Patrick Hart, OCSO
6 x 9, 224 pp, b/w photos, Quality PB, 978-1-893361-49-2 **$16.95**

Waking Up: A Week Inside a Zen Monastery *by Jack Maguire; Foreword by John Daido Loori, Roshi*
6 x 9, 224 pp, b/w photos, Quality PB, 978-1-893361-55-3 **$16.95**; HC, 978-1-893361-13-3 **$21.95**

Spirituality

Next to Godliness: Finding the Sacred in Housekeeping *Edited and with Introductions by Alice Peck*
Offers new perspectives on how we can reach out for the Divine.
6 x 9, 224 pp, Quality PB, 978-1-59473-214-0 **$19.99**

Bread, Body, Spirit: Finding the Sacred in Food *Edited and with Introductions by Alice Peck*
Explores how food feeds our faith. 6 x 9, 224 pp, Quality PB, 978-1-59473-242-3 **$19.99**

Renewal in the Wilderness: A Spiritual Guide to Connecting with God in the Natural World
by John Lionberger Reveals the power of experiencing God's presence in many variations of the natural
world. 6 x 9, 176 pp, b/w photos, Quality PB, 978-1-59473-219-5 **$16.99**

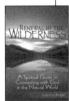

Honoring Motherhood: Prayers, Ceremonies and Blessings
Edited and with Introductions by Lynn L. Caruso
Journey through the seasons of motherhood. 5 x 7¼, 272 pp, HC, 978-1-59473-239-3 **$19.99**

Soul Fire: Accessing Your Creativity *by Rev. Thomas Ryan, CSP*
Learn to cultivate your creative spirit. 6 x 9, 160 pp, Quality PB, 978-1-59473-243-0 **$16.99**

Technology & Spirituality: How the Information Revolution Affects Our Spiritual Lives
by Stephen K. Spyker 6 x 9, 176 pp, HC, 978-1-59473-218-8 **$19.99**

Money and the Way of Wisdom: Insights from the Book of Proverbs
by Timothy J. Sandoval, PhD 6 x 9, 192 pp (est), Quality PB, 978-1-59473-245-4 **$16.99**

Awakening the Spirit, Inspiring the Soul: 30 Stories of Interspiritual Discovery in the
Community of Faiths *Edited by Brother Wayne Teasdale and Martha Howard, MD; Foreword by Joan Borysenko, PhD*
6 x 9, 224 pp, HC, 978-1-59473-039-9 **$21.99**

Creating a Spiritual Retirement: A Guide to the Unseen Possibilities in Our Lives
by Molly Srode 6 x 9, 208 pp, b/w photos, Quality PB, 978-1-59473-050-4 **$14.99** HC, 978-1-893361-75-1 **$19.95**

Finding Hope: Cultivating God's Gift of a Hopeful Spirit
by Marcia Ford 8 x 8, 200 pp, Quality PB, 978-1-59473-211-9 **$16.99**

The Geography of Faith: Underground Conversations on Religious, Political and Social Change
by Daniel Berrigan and Robert Coles 6 x 9, 224 pp, Quality PB, 978-1-893361-40-9 **$16.95**

Jewish Spirituality: A Brief Introduction for Christians *by Lawrence Kushner*
5½ x 8½, 112 pp, Quality PB, 978-1-58023-150-3 **$12.95** *(a Jewish Lights book)*

Journeys of Simplicity: Traveling Light with Thomas Merton, Bashō, Edward Abbey, Annie Dillard & Others
by Philip Harnden 5 x 7¼, 144 pp, Quality PB, 978-1-59473-181-5 **$12.99** 128 pp, HC, 978-1-893361-76-8 **$16.95**

Keeping Spiritual Balance As We Grow Older: More than 65 Creative Ways to
Use Purpose, Prayer, and the Power of Spirit to Build a Meaningful Retirement
by Molly and Bernie Srode 8 x 8, 224 pp, Quality PB, 978-1-59473-042-9 **$16.99**

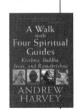

Spirituality 101: The Indispensable Guide to Keeping—or Finding—Your Spiritual Life on Campus
by Harriet L. Schwartz, with contributions from college students at nearly thirty campuses across the United States
6 x 9, 272 pp, Quality PB, 978-1-59473-000-9 **$16.99**

Spiritually Incorrect: Finding God in All the *Wrong* Places *by Dan Wakefield; Illus. by Marian DelVecchio*
5½ x 8½, 192 pp, b/w illus., Quality PB, 978-1-59473-137-2 **$15.99**

Spiritual Manifestos: Visions for Renewed Religious Life in America from Young Spiritual Leaders of Many
Faiths *Edited by Niles Elliot Goldstein; Preface by Martin E. Marty* 6 x 9, 256 pp, HC, 978-1-893361-09-6 **$21.95**

A Walk with Four Spiritual Guides: Krishna, Buddha, Jesus, and Ramakrishna
by Andrew Harvey 5½ x 8½, 192 pp, 10 b/w photos & illus., Quality PB, 978-1-59473-138-9 **$15.99**

What Matters: Spiritual Nourishment for Head and Heart
by Frederick Franck 5 x 7¼, 128 pp, 50+ b/w illus., HC, 978-1-59473-013-9 **$16.99**

Who Is My God?, 2nd Edition: An Innovative Guide to Finding Your Spiritual Identity
Created by the Editors at SkyLight Paths 6 x 9, 160 pp, Quality PB, 978-1-59473-014-6 **$15.99**

Spiritual Practice

Soul Fire: Accessing Your Creativity *by Rev. Thomas Ryan, CSP*
Shows you how to cultivate your creative spirit as a way to encourage personal growth.
6 x 9, 160 pp, Quality PB, 978-1-59473-243-0 **$16.99**

Running—The Sacred Art: Preparing to Practice *by Dr. Warren A. Kay; Foreword by Kristin Armstrong*
Examines how your daily run can enrich your spiritual life. 5½ x 8½, 160 pp, Quality PB, 978-1-59473-227-0 **$16.99**

Hospitality—The Sacred Art: Discovering the Hidden Spiritual Power of Invitation and
Welcome *by Rev. Nanette Sawyer; Foreword by Rev. Dirk Ficca*
Explores how this ancient spiritual practice can transform your relationships.
5½ x 8½, 192 pp, Quality PB, 978-1-59473-228-7 **$16.99**

Thanking & Blessing—The Sacred Art: Spiritual Vitality through Gratefulness
by Jay Marshall, PhD; Foreword by Philip Gulley
Offers practical tips for uncovering the blessed wonder in our lives—even in trying circumstances.
5½ x 8½, 176 pp, Quality PB, 978-1-59473-231-7 **$16.99**

Everyday Herbs in Spiritual Life: A Guide to Many Practices
by Michael J. Caduto; Foreword by Rosemary Gladstar Explores the power of herbs.
7 x 9, 208 pp, 21 b/w illustrations, Quality PB, 978-1-59473-174-7 **$16.99**

Divining the Body: Reclaim the Holiness of Your Physical Self   *by Jan Phillips*
8 x 8, 256 pp, Quality PB, 978-1-59473-080-1 **$16.99**

Finding Time for the Timeless: Spirituality in the Workweek *by John McQuiston II*
Simple stories show you how refocus your daily life. 5½ x 6¾, 208 pp, HC, 978-1-59473-035-1 **$17.99**

The Gospel of Thomas: A Guidebook for Spiritual Practice
by Ron Miller; Translations by Stevan Davies 6 x 9, 160 pp, Quality PB, 978-1-59473-047-4 **$14.99**

Earth, Water, Fire, and Air: Essential Ways of Connecting to Spirit
by Cait Johnson 6 x 9, 224 pp, HC, 978-1-893361-65-2 **$19.95**

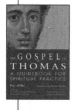

Labyrinths from the Outside In: Walking to Spiritual Insight—A Beginner's Guide
by Donna Schaper and Carole Ann Camp 6 x 9, 208 pp, b/w illus. and photos, Quality PB, 978-1-893361-18-8 **$16.95**

Practicing the Sacred Art of Listening: A Guide to Enrich Your Relationships
and Kindle Your Spiritual Life—The Listening Center Workshop
by Kay Lindahl 8 x 8, 176 pp, Quality PB, 978-1-893361-85-0 **$16.95**

Releasing the Creative Spirit: Unleash the Creativity in Your Life
by Dan Wakefield 7 x 10, 256 pp, Quality PB, 978-1-893361-36-2 **$16.95**

The Sacred Art of Bowing: Preparing to Practice
by Andi Young 5½ x 8½, 128 pp, b/w illus., Quality PB, 978-1-893361-82-9 **$14.95**

The Sacred Art of Chant: Preparing to Practice
by Ana Hernández 5½ x 8½, 192 pp, Quality PB, 978-1-59473-036-8 **$15.99**

The Sacred Art of Fasting: Preparing to Practice
by Thomas Ryan, CSP 5½ x 8½, 192 pp, Quality PB, 978-1-59473-078-8 **$15.99**

The Sacred Art of Forgiveness: Forgiving Ourselves and Others through God's Grace *by Marcia Ford*
8 x 8, 176 pp, Quality PB, 978-1-59473-175-4 **$16.99**

The Sacred Art of Listening: Forty Reflections for Cultivating a Spiritual Practice
by Kay Lindahl; Illustrations by Amy Schnapper 8 x 8, 160 pp, b/w illus., Quality PB, 978-1-893361-44-7 **$16.99**

The Sacred Art of Lovingkindness: Preparing to Practice
by Rabbi Rami Shapiro; Foreword by Marcia Ford 5½ x 8½, 176 pp, Quality PB, 978-1-59473-151-8 **$16.99**

Sacred Speech: A Practical Guide for Keeping Spirit in Your Speech
by Rev. Donna Schaper 6 x 9, 176 pp, Quality PB, 978-1-59473-068-9 **$15.99** HC, 978-1-893361-74-4 **$21.95**

Spirituality & Crafts

The Knitting Way
A Guide to Spiritual Self-Discovery
by Linda Skolnik and Janice MacDaniels
Examines how you can explore and strengthen your spiritual life through knitting.
7 x 9, 240 pp, Quality PB, b/w photographs, 978-1-59473-079-5 **$16.99**

The Scrapbooking Journey
A Hands-On Guide to Spiritual Discovery
by Cory Richardson-Lauve; Foreword by Stacy Julian
Reveals how this craft can become a practice used to deepen and shape your life.
7 x 9, 176 pp, Quality PB, 8-page full-color insert, plus b/w photographs, 978-1-59473-216-4 **$18.99**

The Painting Path
Embodying Spiritual Discovery through Yoga, Brush and Color
by Linda Novick; Foreword by Richard Segalman
Explores the divine connection you can experience through creativity.
7 x 9, 208 pp, 8-page full-color insert, plus b/w photographs, Quality PB, 978-1-59473-226-3 **$18.99**

The Quilting Path
A Guide to Spiritual Discovery through Fabric, Thread and Kabbalah
by Louise Silk
Explores how to cultivate personal growth through quilt making.
7 x 9, 192 pp, Quality PB, b/w photographs and illustrations, 978-1-59473-206-5 **$16.99**

Contemplative Crochet
A Hands-On Guide for Interlocking Faith and Craft
by Cindy Crandall-Frazier; Foreword by Linda Skolnik
Illuminates the spiritual lessons you can learn through crocheting.
7 x 9, 192 pp (est), b/w photographs, Quality PB, 978-1-59473-238-6 **$16.99**

Kabbalah / Enneagram
(from Jewish Lights Publishing)

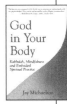

God in Your Body: Kabbalah, Mindfulness and Embodied Spiritual Practice
by Jay Michaelson 6 x 9, Quality PB Original, 978-1-58023-304-0 **$18.99**

Cast in God's Image: Discover Your Personality Type Using the Enneagram and Kabbalah
by Rabbi Howard A. Addison 7 x 9, 176 pp, Quality PB, 978-1-58023-124-4 **$16.95**

Ehyeh: A Kabbalah for Tomorrow *by Dr. Arthur Green*
6 x 9, 224 pp, Quality PB, 978-1-58023-213-5 **$16.99**

The Enneagram and Kabbalah, 2nd Edition: Reading Your Soul
by Rabbi Howard A. Addison 6 x 9, 192 pp, Quality PB, 978-1-58023-229-6 **$16.99**

The Gift of Kabbalah: Discovering the Secrets of Heaven, Renewing Your Life on Earth
by Tamar Frankiel, PhD 6 x 9, 256 pp, Quality PB, 978-1-58023-141-1 **$16.95**
HC, 978-1-58023-108-4 **$21.95**

Kabbalah: A Brief Introduction for Christians
by Tamar Frankiel, PhD 5½ x 8½, 176 pp, Quality PB, 978-1-58023-303-3 **$16.99**

Zohar: Annotated & Explained *Translation and Annotation by Dr. Daniel C. Matt*
Foreword by Andrew Harvey 5½ x 8½, 176 pp, Quality PB, 978-1-893361-51-5 **$15.99**
(a SkyLight Paths book)

About SKYLIGHT PATHS Publishing

SkyLight Paths Publishing is creating a place where people of different spiritual traditions come together for challenge and inspiration, a place where we can help each other understand the mystery that lies at the heart of our existence.

Through spirituality, our religious beliefs are increasingly becoming a part of our lives—rather than *apart* from our lives. While many of us may be more interested than ever in spiritual growth, we may be less firmly planted in traditional religion. Yet, we do want to deepen our relationship to the sacred, to learn from our own as well as from other faith traditions, and to practice in new ways.

SkyLight Paths sees both believers and seekers as a community that increasingly transcends traditional boundaries of religion and denomination—people wanting to learn from each other, *walking together, finding the way.*

For your information and convenience, at the back of this book we have provided a list of other SkyLight Paths books you might find interesting and useful. They cover the following subjects:

Buddhism / Zen	Gnosticism	Mysticism
Catholicism	Hinduism /	Poetry
Children's Books	Vedanta	Prayer
Christianity	Inspiration	Religious Etiquette
Comparative Religion	Islam / Sufism	Retirement
Current Events	Judaism	Spiritual Biography
Earth-Based Spirituality	Kabbalah	Spiritual Direction
Enneagram	Meditation	Spirituality
Global Spiritual	Midrash Fiction	Women's Interest
Perspectives	Monasticism	Worship

Or phone, fax, mail or e-mail to: SKYLIGHT PATHS Publishing
Sunset Farm Offices, Route 4 • P.O. Box 237 • Woodstock, Vermont 05091
Tel: (802) 457-4000 • Fax: (802) 457-4004 • www.skylightpaths.com
Credit card orders: (800) 962-4544 (8:30AM–5:30PM ET Monday–Friday)
Generous discounts on quantity orders. SATISFACTION GUARANTEED. Prices subject to change.